John R. (John Roy) Musick

Stories of Missouri

John R. (John Roy) Musick

Stories of Missouri

ISBN/EAN: 9783337005580

Printed in Europe, USA, Canada, Australia, Japan

Cover: Foto ©Andreas Hilbeck / pixelio.de

More available books at **www.hansebooks.com**

STORIES OF MISSOURI

BY

JOHN R. MUSICK
AUTHOR OF "THE COLUMBIAN HISTORICAL NOVELS"

NEW YORK ∴ CINCINNATI ∴ CHICAGO
AMERICAN BOOK COMPANY
1897

Copyright, 1897, by
AMERICAN BOOK COMPANY.

STO. OF MO.

W. P. 1

PREFACE.

The early inhabitants of Missouri were a peculiar people. First of all were the Indians. When they settled there, no one knows. Next came the French, then the Spaniards, and lastly the Americans. The last named were mostly from Kentucky, Tennessee, and Virginia.

Nearly all the American settlers in Missouri were the descendants of pioneers who had grown accustomed to the trying scenes of forest life. They were a rigidly honest people. No locks were on their doors, and they had no need of any.

As they were dependent on each other for protection, what belonged to one was freely loaned to his neighbor. If a pioneer wanted to borrow his neighbor's ax, and did not find the man at home, he took the ax without asking, and returned it when done with it.

The early Missourians were rude and uncultured, but unselfish and brave. Stories of them, and of the people who preceded and followed them, are both entertaining and instructive. They serve to explain many curious names, customs, and laws, which to a person unfamiliar with the people must remain a mystery.

In the preparation of these stories, the author received valuable aid from the following persons: Dr. Willis P. King, author of "Stories of a Country Doctor"; Honorable A. A. Lesueur, Secretary of State for Missouri; Honorable J. A. Wickham, Adjutant General; Professor J. R. Kirk, State Superintendent of Public Schools; Professor J. M. Greenwood of Kansas City; Major J. B. Merwin of St. Louis; and Professor C. E. Ross, Secretary of the North Missouri State Normal School. Also from Colonel W. F. Switzler's "History of Missouri."

Many of these stories have in some form been in print before, but there are a number that appear for the first time. Care has been taken to select those typical of the time, characteristic of the people, and unquestionably true; also to select such as throw some light on the history of Missouri.

The author trusts that this little volume may stimulate his young readers to learn more of the great State in which they live. They can never become good citizens without having some knowledge of their own State and the people who founded it.

CONTENTS.

1. FRENCH AND SPANISH PERIOD.

		PAGE
I.	Father Marquette	9
II.	The Explorations of La Salle	14
III.	The Silver Hunter	19
IV.	The First Settlers	24
V.	Pierre Laclède, and the Hunter	32
VI.	French Missourians	39
VII.	Attack on St. Louis	45
VIII.	Daniel Boone in Missouri	53
IX.	Maturin Bouvet and the Osages	59

2. TERRITORIAL PERIOD.

X.	Louisiana Purchase	66
XI.	The First Schoolmasters	72
XII.	Early Missourians	78
XIII.	Western Boatmen	86
XIV.	The Blockhouse at the Big Spring	96
XV.	The Lewis and Clark Expedition	101
XVI.	Pike in Northeast Missouri	108
XVII.	Captain Cole. — A Plucky Frenchwoman	112
XVIII.	Missouri Rangers	118
XIX.	The Captive	125
XX.	Boone's Salt Works	130
XXI.	Cooper and Callaway	136
XXII.	The Earthquake at New Madrid	143

		PAGE
XXIII.	Missouri Territory	151
XXIV.	Fanatical Pilgrims	157
XXV.	The Early Lawyer	163

3. EARLY STATE PERIOD.

XXVI.	Thomas H. Benton	171
XXVII.	Some Customs and People of the Past	176
XXVIII.	The New Capital	183
XXIX.	The Big Neck War. — The Platte Purchase	188
XXX.	The Mormons	196
XXXI.	The Honey War. — Colonel Gentry	208
XXXII.	Doniphan and Price	214

4. CIVIL WAR PERIOD.

XXXIII.	Border Trouble	223
XXXIV.	A Season of Doubt	232
XXXV.	Camp Jackson	237
XXXVI.	A Governor's Flight	245
XXXVII.	A Hero's Death	250
XXXVIII.	War in the North	257
XXXIX.	Order Number Eleven	264
XL.	End of the War	272

5. PRESENT PERIOD.

XLI.	The Ironclad Oath	277
XLII.	Restoration of Prosperity	281

STORIES OF MISSOURI.

I.

FATHER MARQUETTE.

ONE hundred and thirty-two years after De Soto discovered the Mississippi River there lived in Canada two great explorers. One was a priest known in history as Father Marquette; the other, a fur trader named Robert de La Salle. Canada then belonged to France, and these explorers were Frenchmen.

Three great European powers had at this time planted colonies in North America. The English colonies were along the Atlantic coast, the Spanish were confined to Florida and Mexico, and most of the French settlements were in Lower Canada. All the great country now known as the Mississippi valley was unexplored, and no one lived there except wandering tribes of Indian savages.

Marquette and La Salle had heard of the mighty river from the Indians, and determined to go into the wilderness in search of it. They did not start together, and it is doubtful if one knew what the other's intentions were, for their paths in life were quite different.

The first to reach the Mississippi was the priest. Father Marquette was a good man. He did not come to the New World to gain riches, fame, or power, as did many others. He had heard that there were heathen in America who knew not the true God, and his mission to the wilderness was to teach them of the Great Being who made us. For five years he had been working in the region of the Great Lakes, and for the last two years his station was at the foot of Lake Michigan.

The Indians talked very freely with Marquette about the great river and wilderness which the white men had not yet seen. In this manner they kindled within his breast a desire to visit the tribes which lived in that country. In the year 1673, with a small party, he set out on his remarkable journey.

One of the men who went with him was a Frenchman named Joliet. This explorer was not a priest, like Father Marquette, but an ambitious man. He too was eager to see the great river and the vast country it drained, but he cared little about converting the Indians to Christianity. His object was to extend the territory and power of his king.

Marquette and Joliet embarked on Lake Michigan in birch-bark canoes, and made their way up Green Bay and Fox River to the watershed between the Mississippi and the Lakes. Then by crossing a short portage they reached the Wisconsin River. The country between the Wisconsin and the head waters of the Fox was a wild prairie, over which the boatmen were compelled to carry their light boats on their shoulders.

Embarking on the bosom of the Wisconsin, the men

drifted down the stream in their canoes. On June 17, 1673, they discovered the Mississippi at the mouth of the Wisconsin. They then began their voyage down the larger stream. From time to time they landed and searched for Indians, but for a long time saw no sign of any. One day, when they had brought their boats near the shore, Joliet pointed to the sandy bank and said, —

"There are some footprints!"

Father Marquette glanced in the direction indicated by Joliet's finger, and saw that a path had been made up the sloping bank. The priest ordered the boats to land, and went on shore.

"Here is a path leading through the woods," he said. "Let us follow it."

Joliet was a bold man, but for a moment he hesitated. The priest, however, knew no fear, and his companion was soon induced to accompany him and the interpreters along the well-beaten path. About six miles from the river they came upon an Indian village. The savages were surprised at first; but when the interpreters made themselves known, they received the travelers very kindly, gave them some dried venison, and told them much about the country.

One of the chiefs gave Marquette a calumet. This was a pipe with a stone bowl and a stem ornamented with eagle's feathers. It was an emblem of peace. He was told that he would meet hostile Indians on his way, and that if he held up the calumet they would not harm him, but treat him as a friend.

Marquette and Joliet were advised, however, not to proceed down the river, for below there was a great demon which would devour them if they persisted in their journey. Despite this warning, they resumed their voyage as before. The only demons that they found were some strange paintings on a rocky bluff.

Continuing down the Mississippi, supported by food obtained from the Indians along the shore, they reached the mouth of the Missouri River, where they landed. Unless De Soto or some of his party entered the territory of what is now Missouri (which is doubted by some), Marquette and his followers were the first white men that did so.

That great, dark stream which flowed into the Mississippi was called by Father Marquette Pekitanoui (pek-i-tan-o-wee), meaning " Muddy Water." The river was known as Muddy Water until 1712, when it was named Missouri from a tribe of Indians who inhabited the country at its mouth.

Resuming their voyage, the explorers floated some distance below the mouth of the Missouri, and beyond the present limits of the State. One day they discovered a number of Indians armed with clubs and bows and arrows, coming toward them in canoes. They saw at once that the party was hostile. The little band of adventurers were unable to defend themselves against so great odds, and their situation was desperate.

When the Indians had come almost within bowshot, Father Marquette rose in his boat and held aloft the calumet. That emblem of peace was recognized, and the savages finally surrounded the white men as friends.

The travelers were then taken to an Indian village, where they were kindly entertained as long as they wished to stay. Marquette and Joliet gave their hosts some presents, which strengthened the bond of friendship. As they were not prepared to explore the river to its mouth, they now turned about and went back to the settlements in Canada, having satisfied themselves that the great river flowed into the Gulf of Mexico.

About two years later the priest died while on a journey in the wilderness. He had but two companions with him at the time. One supported his head, while the other held a crucifix before his eyes as long as he could see. He was buried in the forest on the shore of Lake Michigan.

II.

THE EXPLORATIONS OF LA SALLE.

WHILE Marquette and Joliet were exploring the Mississippi, the fur trader, La Salle, was trying to raise a force for the same purpose.

La Salle was a brave, ambitious, and persevering man. He was eager to extend the power of France, in the hope that by so doing he might increase his own riches and honors. The stories told by the Indians fired him with a determination to find the great river of which he had read in the old Spanish chronicles, and to take possession of it in the name of his king.

The earliest French explorers had a wrong idea of the course of the Mississippi River. From what they could gather from the natives, they thought that it flowed into the Pacific, and that it would thus afford a passage to China. Such a passage would have been of great advantage to French merchants in trading with that country, since it would shorten the distance their ships had to sail, by many thousands of miles.

With a party of his countrymen, La Salle set out from Montreal, by way of Lake Ontario, to find the Mississippi. His followers did not possess stout hearts like his own, and when they had marched a few days into the great forest, they began to wish themselves safely back in their settlements again.

There were many dangers surrounding them. Not only was the wily Indian ever ready to slay them, but the dense forests abounded in bears, panthers, and poisonous reptiles, which were a constant menace to their safety.

"Let us return," they implored La Salle, "or else we shall wander so far that we shall be lost in the forest and never find our way home again."

But La Salle thundered back, "I will go on!" in a voice of such determination that his followers knew it was useless to try to dissuade him. They thereupon held a consultation among themselves, and that night they one and all deserted him.

On waking next morning La Salle found only the Indian guide with him. But he was so brave and so determined, that with this single companion he pushed on through the wilderness until he reached the Ohio River. He had gone too far east to strike the Missouri or the Mississippi.

While he was trying to explore the Ohio to its mouth, his one remaining companion deserted him. He was now alone in an unknown wilderness, and, realizing how useless and hopeless it was to attempt to explore that vast country unaided, he turned about and wandered back to Montreal.

La Salle did not despair. He went to France, and some years later secured aid and authority from the king to explore the great river and take possession of it in his name. From the course of the tributaries of the stream which he had seen, as well as from the report of Marquette, La Salle became convinced that the great

Mississippi was not an outlet to China, but flowed into the Gulf of Mexico.

On his return to Canada, in 1678, he secured men and supplies, built a ship on the Niagara River, and sailed up Lake Erie and Lake Huron to the foot of Lake Michigan. Then the ship was sent back, and the men made their way southward to the head of the lake in canoes.

In December, 1679, with a party consisting of thirty-three men, La Salle embarked in eight canoes on the St. Joseph River in Michigan. They sailed up the stream a number of miles, then crossed the snow-covered plain by a long portage to the source of the Kankakee River, and then floated down this till they reached the Illinois. Here at a point below Peoria Lake they went into camp and built a fort. The Illinois Indians, because of mistreatment by some French traders, had become very hostile, and for some time it seemed as if the expedition would be a failure. But La Salle made a treaty with them, by which he promised to protect them against their enemies.

It became necessary for La Salle to make a trip from his fort on the Illinois to Canada for more supplies, and to look after some of his affairs, which were in a very confused state. On reaching Montreal, he made a last effort to appease his creditors and borrow money for his new equipment. He succeeded; but soon came the news that the men left in the fort had deserted him. Undismayed, he once more gathered a band of followers and set out for the Illinois by the same dreary route through lake, river, and forest.

La Salle's original plan was to build a large vessel with which to explore the Mississippi, but he had not obtained sufficient money and implements to construct such a craft, and the desertion of his men put an end to the enterprise. This time, therefore, he decided to make the trip down the stream in canoes.

With twenty Frenchmen and twenty-eight Indians, he ascended the Chicago River, crossed a portage, and

embarked on the Illinois River, in these rude boats. It was early in 1682, nine years after the priest Marquette had discovered the Mississippi and Missouri. The weather was very cold, and the men suffered much; but with the determined perseverance so characteristic of La Salle, they continued their voyage down the stream.

At the mouth of the Illinois, they entered the Mississippi River; then, continuing down, they reached the mouth of the Missouri. Here they landed and rested for a short time. Again white men were in what is now the State of Missouri.

La Salle was earnestly warned by the Indians not to proceed further down the river, and was told that there was a great demon below that would destroy him; but he was not the man to be frightened at such tales.

With his followers, he explored the Mississippi to its very mouth, confirming his opinion that it flowed into the Gulf of Mexico. On April 9, 1682, La Salle in a formal manner took possession of the whole Mississippi valley, in the name of the King of France.

In honor of Louis XIV., the reigning king, the explorer named the new territory Louisiana. What is now known as Missouri formed a part of that great country, as did all the territory between the Mississippi and the Rocky Mountains; and for more than a hundred years afterwards this region was called by the name Louisiana.

Five years later, La Salle met his death in the wilderness of Texas, while leading a small party through that country. He became involved in a quarrel with his men, and was shot from ambush by one of them, named Duhaut.

III.

THE SILVER HUNTER.

ABOUT thirty-five years after La Salle took possession of Louisiana for France, the region was placed under the control of a company of traders and speculators, known as the Mississippi Company. New Orleans was built and was for a long time the chief town in the Mississippi valley; and gradually trading posts and forts, which afterwards became settlements and towns, were established farther up the river. Two of the most important of these, Kaskaskia and Fort Chartres, were in what is now known as Illinois. At that time, however, this name was given to a much larger région, Missouri itself being included in what was called the Illinois District.

One of the directors of the Mississippi Company was Sieur Renault (sometimes spelled Renaud), the son of a celebrated iron founder of France. Renault was already a rich man, but, being of an adventurous spirit and having heard much of the New World, he determined to try his fortunes there. It was believed by him, and by many others of his time, that there were rich gold and silver mines in Missouri. Perhaps this belief was founded on the traditions of the Indians.

In 1719, Renault, with two hundred miners and

mechanics, sailed from France to America. He stopped at Santo Domingo on his way, and purchased a large number of slaves for working the mines. Some historians say he bought five hundred.

These slaves were mostly negroes who had been brought by the Spaniards from Africa to work in their gold and silver mines in Santo Domingo. Renault did not linger long on his way, for next year (1720) he was at Fort Chartres, on the Illinois side of the Mississippi River, about ten miles above the present site of Ste. Genevieve, Missouri.

The wild shores on the Missouri side, with their high hills, bluffs, and deep forests, seemed to his imagination filled with hidden treasure; and from Fort Chartres he sent frequent expeditions over into what is now Missouri to explore for silver.

Not receiving any satisfactory report from his men, he himself crossed the river with a party, among whom was a man named La Motte, a relative of the acting governor of the company. They journeyed far into the wilderness, braving many dangers, and digging wherever they thought silver might be found.

One day, while Renault was in advance with a party of slaves and prospectors, they were attacked by a large brown bear, which charged on them with great fury. Renault's companions fled, but he himself remained near a tree, and when the ferocious beast was quite close, leveled his gun and shot it in the brain.

Hearing the report of the gun, the men came back and found the silver hunter standing over the dead bear.

"You have done a great thing," said one of the miners; "you have slain a monster bear."

"Yes," replied Renault, "but had I depended on you, it might have slain me."

Though the followers of Renault were ashamed of their conduct, they had such dread of the forest, that they could hardly be persuaded to venture further. But they were soon joined by La Motte, who with a few miners and slaves had been separated from the rest for several days; and the whole party then continued their explorations together.

They prosecuted their search for silver with great diligence. Nearly all of what is now Ste. Genevieve County was explored by them. Shafts were sunk and mines opened. Lead was found in abundance, but practically no silver. Many of Renault's old mines, overgrown with trees and covered with moss, have been rediscovered by more recent explorers.

One, the "Mine La Motte," is still operated, and is still known by the name its discoverers gave it. It is beyond question the oldest mine in Missouri.

One day some of Renault's miners, who had been on a prospecting tour, told him of a wonderful cavern they had found. The silver hunter set out with them to see it. Reaching a rocky ledge, the prospectors led him into the entrance of an immense cave.

They had with them some pine knots for torches; and, lighting these, they proceeded to explore the wonderful place. They first came to a vast underground chamber. A succession of passages led from this, and in them were millions of pounds of lead ore adhering to the sides, roof, and bottom. Not only did the men discover lead, but zinc and iron ores also, although these were not present in so large quantities as the lead.

This cavern is to-day known as the "Valle Mines," and is among the richest lead-producing mines in Missouri. It was named for one of the early settlers in Ste. Genevieve, of whom we shall hear later. Renault and his companions did not attempt to work it, as they had other mines more convenient to Fort Chartres.

Failing to find silver in paying quantities, Renault became disheartened. One evening, as he sat by the camp fire, lamenting his failure, a companion asked, —

"Why don't you dig for lead? You would get more silver for it than you will ever find in these rocks and hills."

The idea struck the silver hunter very favorably, and he determined at once to act upon it. Next day he proceeded to open up two mines, and set his slaves to taking out lead ore; and he also constructed rude furnaces for smelting it. Before long a number of other mines were opened and worked quite extensively; but just how many were operated by Sieur Renault and his miners is not positively known.

After the lead had been smelted and separated from the dross, it was carried away on pack horses. The pack saddle in that day was a very rude affair. It was built on a forked stick, placed so that one fork came down on each side of the horse. Suspended from this were large pockets of leather, which would hold as much as the animal could carry.

When the pack horses were loaded, a whole caravan

of them was sent in charge of a man or boy along the narrow path through the forest to the river opposite Fort Chartres. The lead was then taken across the

river in boats, while driver and pack horses returned to the mines and furnaces for more.

From Fort Chartres the lead was sent down the Mississippi to New Orleans, and afterwards was conveyed to France. Just how much lead was produced in Missouri in those early days is not known. Some writers say the amount was small, some that it was considerable.

Renault failed to find silver, but he will ever be remembered as the first man who carried on a productive enterprise in Missouri. He opened mines for an ore of greater value to mankind than silver.

IV.

THE FIRST SETTLERS.

ABOUT the year 1730, there lived at Fort Chartres, in Illinois, two Frenchmen, named Francis and Jean Baptiste Valle. These men were brothers, and were noted for their honesty, kindness, and bravery. While members of the Mississippi Company and others from New Orleans and France were searching the rocks and hills of Missouri for gold and silver, these brothers and some friends were traveling through that country, trading with the Indians.

They gave the Indians blankets, hatchets, beads, trinkets, and other things valued by the savages, and received in exchange various kinds of furs. When they traveled on water, they loaded their boats with such merchandise as was suitable for their trade, and paddled along the streams. Sometimes they would be several days going from one Indian village to another. When they arrived at one, either Francis or his brother stood up in the boat, holding in one hand a calumet, and in the other some article of traffic. These meant peace and a desire to trade. Then they would land, and transact their business by means of an interpreter whom they had with them.

But they did not always travel by water. Sometimes

they loaded their goods on pack horses, and went several days' journey into the forests of Missouri, visiting far-off tribes. When a large number of valuable furs had been collected, they were sent down the river to New Orleans, and from there taken in ships to France.

These early traders were very much pleased with the country on the west side of the river, and began to think seriously of crossing over and establishing a trading post there. The soil was fertile, and the Indians were peaceable. A trading post in Missouri, they reasoned, would be much more convenient than Fort Chartres.

Accordingly, about the year 1735, the Valle brothers and several of their friends crossed the river with their families, and established a post, which in time grew into the town of Ste. Genevieve. Its site, however, was three miles distant from the present town of the same name. The post consisted chiefly of one large blockhouse, in which the commandant lived, and which served as the common storehouse; but there were a few smaller houses as well. The blockhouse was intended also to be a refuge for all the people in case of an attack by Indians; and it was provided with portholes from which to fire upon the assailants.

These were the first settlers in Missouri. Their names, so far as known, were as follows: Francis Valle, commandant of the post; Jean Baptiste Valle, his brother; Joseph Loiselle, Jean Baptiste Maurice, Francis Coleman, Jacques Boyer, Henri Maurice, Parfant Dufour, Louis Boidue, B. N. James, and J. B. T. Pratt.

They were men of simple habits and strong constitutions, as honest as they were hospitable; and they cheerfully adapted themselves to their circumstances. Rich and handsome clothing was unknown to them. The men wore homespun trousers, blue woolen shirts, moccasins, and a coon-skin cap in summer; to this in winter they added buckskin leggings and a hunting shirt made of the skin of some wild animal.

The clothing of the women was equally simple. A dress of calico, a Spanish mantilla thrown over the shoulders, and a handkerchief tied carelessly about the neck — this was the usual attire of a Missouri lady of that day. There was no effort at display. Their homes were rude log huts, with chimneys made of sticks and mud, though some of the better houses had chimneys of stone. Few houses had more than one room, with one door and one window.

Contentment and prosperity blessed these first settlers. The hardships and privations which they suffered in common served but to bind them more closely together. Disputes and lawsuits were almost unknown, and for many years this little settlement formed, as it were, one family. On the death of Francis Valle, the first commandant, his brother Jean Baptiste was selected for that important post. The commandant was the ruler of the little colony. He was the judge and governor in peace, and the leader in time of war. Jean Baptiste Valle was regarded with all the respect of a king, yet his rule was more like a father's than a sovereign's.

The men of the settlement were usually occupied in hunting deer and elk, trapping beaver, mink, and otter, and trading with the Indians. The rifle furnished much of their clothing and most of the food for the family;

for wild game of all kinds was found in abundance. Half a dozen hides could nearly always have been seen tacked up on the outside of the house to dry. But hunting, trapping, and trading were not the only industries of these first settlers. They early discovered that the soil was productive, and began to plant corn and to sow wheat. At first they produced only enough to supply their own wants, but this was the beginning of the great agricultural industry in Missouri.

Their farming implements were of the simplest kind, and were mostly of home make. Their plow, for instance, was made from a forked tree, cut off near the point of branching. One fork was left long enough to serve as a pole to which to attach a yoke of oxen, while the other fork was cut off about two feet from the trunk, and sharpened to pierce the earth. A pair of rude handles were then fastened to the top, and the plow was complete.

The products of the chase, mines, trapping, and trading were sent down the river to New Orleans in barges or flatboats constructed by the settlers, who brought back in return articles needful for their own comfort and for traffic with the Indians.

The voyages down the river were long and tedious, and were attended with great danger. When fathers, brothers, and friends departed on these journeys, it was months before they returned. Hostile Indians often attacked them, and the treacherous stream was filled with hidden snags and sand bars, which sometimes destroyed their boats. But the bold pioneers of Ste. Genevieve braved all these dangers. On reaching

New Orleans they laid their boats along the levees, sought out the French ships which were in the harbor, and exchanged their peltries and lead for such articles as they needed.

After the settlers had finished their trading, the hardest task of all yet lay before them. Going down the stream they usually floated with the current, aided by sweeps or large oars; but the return trip was difficult. A mast was sometimes rigged on each boat, and if the wind was favorable they spread their sails and glided on their way towards home. Often, however, the wind was contrary or the river was crooked, so that they could not use a sail to any advantage. Then they were compelled to cordelle the boat up the stream. The boatmen walked along the shore, and by aid of a long rope pulled the boat after them. One or two were left on board to steer, and keep the prow from running into the bank. In this way many a weary day was passed before they came to the end of their journey.

But the life of the first French settlers in Missouri was not all toil and hardship. They had various kinds of amusements and merrymakings, among which the "king's ball" held an important place. It occurred once a year and was looked forward to with eagerness by both young and old. Every inhabitant of the village was in attendance. One feature of this ball was the cutting and eating of a large cake in which had been placed four beans. Each person getting a bean in his slice was to be one of the "kings" or leaders of the next ball.

Another gathering was known as the "guinolee." This was a masked ball which afforded much amusement. Among the men, old-fashioned "shooting matches" were a favorite sport. These brought about a perfection in marksmanship that has never been excelled, and that was of great advantage to them in their forest life.

History leaves but a brief record of these first settlers. For over half a century little is known of them. In 1785, however, a flood in the Mississippi destroyed the old town of Ste. Genevieve, and the settlers then moved their homes to the present site.

Mingled with the early history of Ste. Genevieve are a number of legends, among which is the story of an Indian maiden whose name is not known. Several years after the settlement had been established, there came to the village a young French trader named Francis Maisonville. While trading with some Indians, he met this Indian maiden and loved her. His love was returned, and they were married by a priest. For some reason the dusky friends of the bride opposed this union, and one day, while the husband was absent, her brother, with some of his companions, seized her and carried her away into the wilderness.

When the husband returned and found his wife gone, he summoned some white friends and set out to overtake the Indians and bring her back. But the cunning savages waded long distances in streams, walked backwards, and used many other devices to conceal their trail and confuse their pursuers as to the course they had taken. After days of fruitless search, the white men gave up the chase in despair, and returned to Ste. Genevieve.

Meanwhile, the bride had been taken to an Indian village about six days' journey from Ste. Genevieve. Here she was kept in an Indian wigwam, guarded by two aged squaws. One night the old women, worn out with watching, fell asleep. A gentle rain was falling, as the prisoner knew by the patter on the wigwam.

Ever watchful for an opportunity to escape, she crawled stealthily to the door. She moved as noiselessly as possible, for all depended upon her not arousing the sleeping women. Her hands and feet were tied with strips of deerskin. Holding her wrists out under the drip from the wigwam, she soon wet the thongs, which were then easily stretched so that she slipped her hands out.

Then she untied her feet, and, after giving the sleeping women a careful glance, ran out into the darkness and rain. She had been gone but a few minutes when her guards awoke and gave the alarm. The brother hastily summoned his fleetest warriors and started in pursuit.

For many days the young bride fled through the forest, subsisting on wild berries and fruits. Sometimes her brother and his friends were so near that she could hear them. One night she crawled into a hollow log to rest. She had been there but a few minutes when she heard the voices of her brother and his warriors close at hand. They built a camp fire near by, and her brother sat on the very log in which she was hiding, while he and his warriors toasted their venison; but so quiet did she remain that they suspected nothing, and at early dawn they departed. When they were gone she crept from her hiding place, and resumed her journey.

At last she reached her home. The husband, almost broken-hearted, was in the cabin when she entered. He was overjoyed to see her, and for fear that her relatives might steal her away again, he took her to live in the blockhouse, or fort. Her brother and relatives after a time became reconciled to the marriage, and were ever after the steadfast friends of young Maisonville.

The Peoria Indians, who lived in the country around Ste. Genevieve, were more industrious than most of the aborigines. They were strong and straight, and fine specimens of manhood. The women were beautiful, and swift on foot. The honesty and fairness with which the first settlers treated the Indians, prevented misunderstanding and war. Justice was practiced by both races, and the colonists long lived by the side of the Indians in peace.

V.

PIERRE LACLÈDE, AND THE HUNTER.

IN November, 1762, France ceded all the vast country then known as Louisiana to Spain. For political reasons, this transaction was kept a profound secret, and the inhabitants of Upper Louisiana did not know of it for several years. The King of France and his officers continued to govern the country as before. In February, 1763, the king ceded to Great Britain all his territory east of the Mississippi, except New Orleans, in spite of the fact that he had previously given a portion of the same country to Spain. This treaty was at once made public, and the people of Louisiana soon heard all about it.

Fort Chartres, in Illinois, had up to this time been the seat of government and the center of trade for Upper Louisiana, or, as it was sometimes called, the Illinois District. According to the treaty, this town was to be surrendered to the British, and so a new location for government and trade had to be selected for the territory west of the Mississippi River.

The colonial treasury was empty, and the government was unable to build a post in the wilderness. Therefore it was decided to give some private company the exclusive right to trade with the Indians, on condition that it should select a site and build the post. This monopoly of the fur trade was to extend throughout the north and northwest of the territory. The firm of Maxent, Laclède & Company received the grant. They fitted out an expedition which left New Orleans August 3, 1763, and wintered at Fort Chartres.

The leader of this expedition was the junior member of the firm, and is known in history as Pierre Laclède, though his full name was Pierre Laclède Ligueste. He was a Frenchman, born in Bion, near the base of the Pyrenees Mountains. Trained as a merchant, he seems to have been possessed of intelligence and foresight, as was shown in his selection of the site for the post.

During the winter of 1763-4, while his men were quartered at Fort Chartres, Laclède explored the west shore of the Mississippi below the mouth of the Missouri. He finally chose as the place for his post the spot where the city of St. Louis now stands. In February, 1764, he sent Auguste Chouteau and a band of workmen to make a clearing and to begin building log cabins at this place. A number of French families crossed over from Fort Chartres, and soon a flourishing settlement was established.

Laclède called his new town St. Louis, in honor of the King of France; for it was not yet known even to the leaders that this territory had passed under Spanish control. He laid it out in regular blocks and streets, some of which still bear the names he gave them. His store was on Main Street, in front of the place where the Merchants' Exchange now stands.

The firm of Maxent, Laclède & Company, sometimes

known as the "Louisiana Fur Company," soon did a thriving business. Almost every day the streets of the little town were filled with Indians, bringing furs to trade for such articles as they wanted. A look into the company's store would astonish one accustomed to modern shops. One would see rifles, powder, bullets,

hatchets, knives, blankets, gay-colored handkerchiefs, and every trinket calculated to please the savage fancy.

In the year 1765 Fort Chartres was surrendered by the French to the British. Captain Sterling was the English officer who took possession of the post. St. Ange de Belle Rive, the French commander of Fort Chartres upon its surrender, removed with his officers and troops to St. Louis on July 17, 1765. From that time the new settlement was considered the capital of Upper Louisiana. Immediately upon his arrival, St. Ange assumed control, though it is doubtful if he had any legal authority to do so.

St. Louis, Ste. Genevieve, and a small settlement at New Madrid were the only white settlements at this time in what is now Missouri; but others soon sprang up on the fertile banks of the Mississippi and Missouri rivers. The mildness of the government, and the liberality with which land grants were made, in addition to the advantages which the trade of the country offered, attracted immigration from Canada and Lower Louisiana.

Vide Poche, afterwards called Carondelet, in honor of the Baron de Carondelet, was founded by Delor de Tregette in 1767. In 1776, Florisant settlement, afterwards called St. Ferdinand, in honor of the King of Spain, was founded by Beaurosier Dunegant. The village which sprang up about the settlement was subsequently named Florisant, while the township in which it is situated is known as St. Ferdinand. These settlements are all in St. Louis County, and Carondelet is to-day a suburb of the city of St. Louis.

The rich alluvial soil of the valley yielded an abundance to the settlers. The Indian fur trade became extensive, and St. Louis rapidly grew into prominence, not only among the French and Spanish, but also among the English, who were now gradually coming across the Alleghanies into the Ohio valley.

Among the earliest French settlers in St. Louis was

a man named Blanchette, a friend of Laclède and Chouteau. He loved the forest, and preferred hunting to cultivating the soil or trading with the Indians; so he came to be called "Blanchette Chasseur," or Blanchette the Hunter. He would spend days alone in the forest with his gun and dogs. On account of rattlesnakes and copperheads, which were abundant, he often climbed into the branches of a tree to sleep.

Once, having chased a wounded deer until darkness came upon him, he looked about for a tree in which to pass the night. A large oak with thick clusters of branches and dense foliage seemed to invite him to repose in its bushy top. He climbed to the first fork and took the most comfortable position he could find. Hanging his rifle by a leather strap on a small branch at his side, he prepared to sleep.

His faithful dogs, which had been following the deer, returned to their master shortly after he was in his strange bed, and set up a tremendous howling. He spoke to them and ordered them away, but all to no purpose. They remained beneath the tree, barking furiously.

"Something is wrong," thought the hunter, "or those dogs would not act in this way."

He crept down from the tree, and with his flint and steel kindled a fire. As the light ascended into the branches, he saw a pair of fiery eyes not ten feet from where he had been resting. The hunter raised his rifle, took aim, and fired. An enormous panther fell, mortally wounded. The dogs leaped on it, and though it was dying, it succeeded in killing one of them.

Blanchette was not only a great marksman, but a

great horseman as well, and many stories are told of his skill with horse and rifle. He was once hunting with an Indian friend when they started up a fine fat buck. The Indian fired and missed.

"Never mind; I will get it for you," said Blanchette; and he galloped away after the deer, which was running toward the river. When the animal reached the water's edge it turned north, whereupon the hunter cut

across through the wood to head it off. He came out within a hundred paces of it, and horse and deer sped along neck and neck. Blanchette dropped the rein, and, raising his rifle, brought down the deer at the first shot without slackening his speed. He gave it to his Indian friend, and an hour later had shot one for himself.

In 1768, attracted by the abundant game north of the Missouri River, he crossed that stream and built a log cabin. The advantages for hunting and trapping here were so much superior to those south of the river, that he induced some friends to join him. In 1769, he established the post of Les Petites Côtes. A fort was built here, and a settlement sprang up around it, — the first in the present State north of the Missouri. The name was afterwards changed from Les Petites Côtes to St. Charles, which is the name it bears to-day.

Thus the cities of St. Louis and St. Charles were founded. Laclède, the founder of St. Louis, died of a fever in June, 1778, while on his way home from New Orleans with a fleet of "keel boats." After his death, Colonel Auguste Chouteau became the owner of his residence. It was enlarged and beautified, and for many years was the finest house in St. Louis.

The fate of Blanchette the Hunter is not positively known. Some think he was killed by the Indians, while others say that he died of sickness in St. Charles, the town which he had founded.

VI.

FRENCH MISSOURIANS.

WHEN Great Britain took possession of the country east of the Mississippi, many of the French families living in Illinois moved to Missouri. By doing so, they supposed that they were still French subjects, for they had not yet heard of the treaty by which Spain acquired all of Louisiana west of the great river.

Although they were too far removed from any nation to be much influenced by political changes, they all preferred the French rule to any other.

In their manner of settling the French differed from all the other European colonists in America. They preferred to gather in compact little villages, instead of making their homes on separate and often distant farms, as was the custom of the English. The French towns were usually to be found on the margin of a prairie or the banks of some river. The streets were long and narrow, with the dwellings so close together that the sociable villagers could converse with their neighbors from their windows and doorways.

Such were the early villages of St. Louis, Ste. Genevieve, and St. Charles, which for some time were the largest settlements in Upper Louisiana. They were small patriarchal hamlets, each like one great family clustered about a parental home. The houses were simple and much alike, being usually one story high, and surrounded by sheds or galleries. The walls were constructed of rude framework, with upright corner posts and studding, connected horizontally by means of numerous cross ties, not unlike the rounds of a ladder. These held the "cat and clay" (hair or grass and mud) with which the intervening spaces were filled, and which formed a sort of plastering for the inside surface. Each homestead was in a separate lot, inclosed by a rude picket fence.

Nearly every village had a common field consisting of hundreds, and often thousands, of acres of uninclosed land. This was free to all for use as a common pasture and for obtaining fuel and timber. In addition to this, each settler had his own field for agriculture.

The French pioneers in Missouri were generally a merry people. One writer says of them,—"Care was a stranger in those early days. Amusements, festivals, and holidays made the people happy and content, though in the wilderness and secluded from the great civilized world. While the young and the gay danced, the aged patriarch and his companion looked on and smiled. Even the priest sanctioned and blessed the innocent amusement and recreation."

Feasting, dancing, and other amusements were not confined to either sex nor to any class. In the dance, all participated, the bond and the free alike. Even the red men and women from the forest often came to share in the revelry.

The Indians regarded the settlers as their friends,

and trusted them fully. The French policy towards them was so fair that Missouri did not suffer from the desolating Indian wars which so frequently ravaged the English colonies. In the treatment of slaves, also, the French were so gentle and kind that a writer of the time says, "The world has never seen a more contented and happy people than the negro slaves of the early French of Upper Louisiana."

Statute books, lawyers, courts, and prisons were unheard of among these first settlers. Every man rendered unto every other his just due; consequently there was no need of them. Hospitality was a duty, and taverns were unknown; for every man's door was open to the traveler and stranger. This social characteristic is well illustrated by the story of an Englishman who came down the river in his boat, and landed at St. Louis. He approached a house in front of which a number of people were gathered, and asked, —

"Is this a tavern?"

"No," was the answer.

The perplexed traveler pointed to another house and asked, —

"Is that a tavern?"

"No."

"Will you show me one?" he asked.

The Englishman was astonished when his informer said, —

"We have none."

"No tavern!" he cried. "Then where am I to sleep to-night, — in my open boat, or under a tree?"

The Frenchman answered, —

"There are many houses here; why not sleep in one of them?"

The traveler then saw that the villagers were offering him the hospitality of their homes. He was entertained that night by Colonel Chouteau. A long war between France and Great Britain had just ended, and the French in Missouri, though removed from the scenes of hostility, had been loyal to the cause of their mother country, and bitterly disliked the English. Nevertheless, Colonel Chouteau looked after the comfort of his guest, and no unpleasant allusions were made to the recent war. The Englishman and Colonel Chouteau were ever after fast friends.

The young men among these early settlers were hunters, trappers, and traders, who rivaled each other in their long journeys on the streams or in the pathless wilderness. Sometimes they were gone from their homes for months, penetrating the most central parts of Missouri. When they returned from their long journeys, laden with furs, they were greeted with smiling faces and the warmest welcome. They often had interesting stories to tell of their wanderings in the forest.

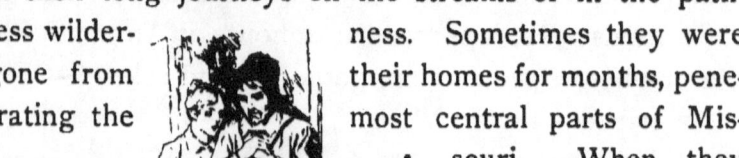

Once two young men crossed the Missouri and wandered far into the wilderness.

When they came back they told of springs of water issuing from the ground, so salty that one could not drink from them. They were a great resort for deer, buffalo, and elk. This place was probably what was afterwards known as Boones Lick, which was at one time famous for its salt works.

Often the return of the *voyageurs*, as these young hunters and traders were called, was celebrated by balls and festivities.

"My son has returned from a great journey in the forest," the father would say. "Let us give him a feast and a ball, and be happy that he is with us again."

Mechanics by profession were almost unknown in the settlements of Missouri. The great business of all was trading with Indians, caring for flocks and herds, and cultivating enough land to supply themselves with food. Every man was his own carpenter, shoemaker, saddler, and mason. If he wanted a house, he built it. It was a rude affair when finished, but it made a comfortable home. The life of these pioneers reminds one of Robinson Crusoe, who, like them, had to build his own house and to make his own boat and clothes.

There were no public schools for many years. The priests at the forts and trading stations sometimes taught the children, Indian and white alike, to read and write, and gave them a little knowledge of mathematics. These mission schools were the exception, however, rather than the rule, and many grew to be women and men incapable of reading or writing even their own names.

The early French settlers did not give much thought to affairs of state. They believed that France was the greatest nation on earth, and trusted to her for protection. They cared nothing for fame, any more than for the luxuries of life.

The peace of this happy people was at last broken by a rumor that all Louisiana had been ceded to Spain. In the hour of doubt and anxiety they appealed to their commandant, St. Ange.

"I know nothing of it," he answered.

But after a while the rumors were confirmed; and finally a courier came up from New Orleans to say that O'Reilly, the Spanish governor, had taken possession of the country. The people in Missouri had no thought of resisting the Spanish government. If Louisiana had really been ceded to Spain, they were willing to abide by the result.

On May 20, 1770, Pedro Piernas, as lieutenant governor of Louisiana, reached St. Louis and superseded St. Ange. The change was made quietly, with little show or parade. Many regretted that France had abandoned them, but all submitted without a murmur. In time, all became reconciled to the change, for the administration of affairs was mild, and there was little cause to complain of the new ruler.

VII.

ATTACK ON ST. LOUIS.

DON PEDRO PIERNAS, the first Spanish lieutenant governor at St. Louis, was an agreeable disappointment. He was a just and kind man, and did everything in his power to assure the French settlers that their private possessions would not be disturbed.

A strong friendship sprang up between him and St. Ange, whom he made a captain of infantry. He appointed Martin Duralde, another Frenchman, surveyor to establish the boundaries of the land grants made by St. Ange, and in a public manner confirmed them.

In 1775, Piernas was succeeded by Francisco Cruzat. This man also was a mild ruler, and followed the policy of his predecessor. He lived in the house which Piernas had occupied during his term of office. This house had once belonged to Laclède, and was situated at the corner of Main and Walnut streets. In 1778, Cruzat was succeeded by Don Fernando de Leyba, a drunken, avaricious, feeble-minded Spaniard whom no one could love or respect.

For three years a great struggle had been going on between Great Britain and her American colonies on the Atlantic coast. A war so far away could affect the people of Missouri but little, and most of them seldom gave it a thought. As the Indians of the great Northwest, however, had taken sides with the British, some of the settlers advocated the policy of remaining strictly neutral, though the sympathies of all were with the colonies.

The avowed sympathy of Spain for the American colonies caused the people of St. Louis some uneasiness. This was increased when Colonel Rogers Clark, the American, captured the British posts at Cahokia, Kaskaskia, and other villages near St. Louis, on the east side of the river. The proximity of one combatant might bring another. Colonel Clark, however, instead of remaining in the vicinity of St. Louis, hastened away to capture the British fort at St. Vincent (now Vincennes, Indiana), and the inhabitants of St. Louis began to breathe freely again.

But Colonel Chouteau argued to his fellow-townsmen that Spanish sympathy with the colonies made St. Louis an object of British and Indian wrath. This opinion was strengthened when rumors reached St. Louis, day after day, that large bodies of Englishmen and Indians were advancing on the town. The colonel and his brother repeatedly called attention to the defenseless condition of the place, and at last efforts were made to fortify it.

A wall of logs and clay was built around it, five feet high, with three gates. The wall was semicircular in form, with the ends terminating at the river. At each of the gates cannon were planted and kept in constant readiness for use. A small fort was also built on what is now Fourth Street, near Walnut; this was afterward used for a prison.

Months passed, and no foe was seen. Winter came and went without any indication of hostilities. Those who had doubted the existence of danger began to twit the more cautious for their extra care in building the fortifications. Even the most apprehensive relaxed their vigilance to some extent. Spring came, and to all appearances peace reigned west of the Mississippi. But in reality the town was soon to be the scene of conflict.

A few years before, a French Canadian named Ducharme had been caught trading with Indians in the Spanish territory. As this was in violation of the Spanish laws, his goods were seized and confiscated. Rankling with resentment, he now helped to bring about an attack on St. Louis by a body of Ojibways, Winnebagoes, Sioux, and other Indians, in all about fifteen hundred, under the leadership of a British officer from Fort Michilimackinac. Some historians say there were also one hundred and fifty English soldiers in the hostile force. This numerous band gathered on the eastern shore of the river, a little above St. Louis, and made arrangements to begin the attack on May 26, 1780.

May 25th was the festival of Corpus Christi, which was celebrated by the Catholic inhabitants with religious ceremonies, feasting, and rejoicing. A number of men, women, and children left the inclosure, and scattered about over the prairie to pick the wild strawberries which grew there in great abundance.

Ducharme, with a part of his Indian force, crossed over that day. Spies were sent through the woods to reconnoiter, but fortunately no attack was made. The commanders of the expedition did not think their force on the west side of the river was strong enough to be successful.

On the following morning, just before dawn, the remainder of the Indians glided across the Mississippi in their canoes, and landed in a dense wood, where is now located the portion of the city called Bremen. They halted long enough to look about and assure themselves that their arrival was unnoticed. Then they made their way back of the village, hoping to find some of the people at work in the fields.

Near where the fair grounds are now situated, there was a spring which was known as Cardinal Spring. Cardinal, the man for whom it was named, and another man, called John Baptiste Riviere, were just at this time near by it, their rifles with them. Cardinal was stooping over for a drink, when Riviere discovered a savage creeping through the tall grass among the trees.

"Indians! Indians!" he cried, and fired.

Cardinal started up and seized his gun, which he had laid at his side. Wild yells rose all around him. He fired, and both Frenchmen then turned to fly. A storm of bullets brought Cardinal bleeding and dying to the ground. Riviere, finding escape impossible, surrendered and was taken to the Chicago River; but in time he succeeded in gaining his freedom, and returned to St. Louis.

There were others outside the fortification. The

firing in the direction of Cardinal Spring was the first intimation they had of the presence of a foe. As soon as they heard it, they started for the fort at the top of their speed. It was a race for life.

The next victim was an old white-haired man. He had been in the field at work when the firing at Cardinal Spring was heard. Dropping his hoe, he ran to the fence, seized his gun, and started for the fort. After passing through a grove of trees, he came upon a strip of prairie that lay between him and the fort. Several shots were here fired at him, but all missed. Half a dozen Indians started to head him off. He fired, and for a moment checked them; but one young warrior, running a little nearer to the old man, leveled his rifle and shot him down.

His death was soon avenged. As the old man fell, a swift-footed young Frenchman with loaded gun was running to his relief. Pausing near the body, the young man took aim and shot the

Indian dead. Then, turning to the fleeing women and children, he cried, —

"Run for your lives, — fly to the fort!" Despite the whizzing of bullets, he proceeded to reload his gun and to cover their flight. Several bullets and arrows struck him before the gun was reloaded. He fired once more, and then fell dead.

Both Colonel Auguste Chouteau and his brother Pierre were in the town at the time of the attack. Knowing that there were many people outside the inclosure, they seized their guns and rushed bravely to the rescue. On the way, they rallied a dozen more armed citizens. When they reached the prairie, a terrible scene met their eyes. Men, women, and children were flying toward the fort, pursued by savages.

"Charge!" cried Colonel Chouteau. With a shout, his gallant little band of followers dashed forward and fired a volley at the pursuing Indians. Three or four dropped under their deadly aim, and the others came to a halt. This gave an opportunity for the remaining fugitives to reach the fort.

The town of St. Louis was in wild confusion. The long-dreaded attack had come at last. Citizens seized their guns and rushed to the defense. Colonel Chouteau and his brother Pierre were the heroes of the day.

"Where are the militia from Ste. Genevieve?" asked some one. This body of troops, under command of Captain Silvia Francisco Cartabona, had been sent from Ste. Genevieve some time before, to protect the town in case of attack. Now they were nowhere to be seen. Colonel Chouteau sent his brother Pierre to find them. The latter returned in a few moments and said that they were hiding in the houses, and that he was unable to bring them to the walls.

"And where is Governor Leyba?" asked the colonel.

"Locked up in his own house, drunk!" answered Pierre.

"Then we have no leader," cried the colonel. "We must defend ourselves."

"You shall be our leader. We will fight under you," shouted the people. They could not have chosen a better commander. Auguste Chouteau was brave, beloved, and trusted. He and his brother, with the most experienced artillerists, managed the cannon.

The Indians rallied, and approached the fort. When they were within a short distance of it, they opened an irregular fire on the gates. From the wall and the tops of the houses, the people returned the fire with rifles and muskets.

The artillerists then poured in volleys of grapeshot and canister, which swept down the red foes and drove them back. This energetic resistance was unexpected. The strength of the fort, and the roar of the cannon, dismayed the savages. Ducharme was wounded, and his Indian allies became discouraged. It was not long before they abandoned the attack, and recrossed the river.

About thirty of the inhabitants of St. Louis were killed. Most of the slain had fallen on the prairie, while trying to reach the fort; many of these were old men, women, and children. About thirty more had been captured and carried away. A number of these were afterward released, and returned to their homes; some, however, were never seen by their friends again.

The cowardly conduct of the lieutenant governor was reported to the authorities at New Orleans, and an appeal was made for his removal. Leyba was therefore recalled, and Cartabona acted in his place until the arrival of Cruzat, who was again appointed lieutenant governor of Upper Louisiana. After Cruzat arrived the fortifications were improved, but the town was not again attacked.

In 1788, Cruzat was succeeded by Manuel Perez, as commandant general of the post of St. Louis and the West Illinois country. In 1793, Perez gave place to Zenon Trudeau, who, in 1799, was succeeded by Charles Dehault Delassus de Delusière, a Frenchman who had been in the service of Spain many years. This man was the last Spanish lieutenant governor.

In 1799, Delassus, as he is usually called, had a census taken of the Upper Louisiana settlements. The result was as follows: Ste. Genevieve, 949; St. Louis, 925; St. Charles, 875; New Madrid, 782; New Bourbon, 560; Cape Girardeau, 521; St. Andrew, 393; Marius des Liard, 376; St. Ferdinand, 276; Carondelet, 184; Meramec, 115; Little Meadows, 72.

VIII.

DANIEL BOONE IN MISSOURI.

ABOUT the year 1797, Daniel Boone, the great hunter and Indian fighter, made up his mind to leave his home and go to Missouri. There were several reasons why the old pioneer decided to take this step, but probably the most important one was the loss of his land.

Daniel Boone was a bold pioneer and hunter, but a man of scant education. He knew but little of the tricks of lawyers, — not enough to protect his own interests. Taking it for granted that every man was honest like himself, he thought that no great knowledge of law was necessary. He had located and entered a large tract of land in Kentucky, but through carelessness and ignorance of law had failed to get his papers properly executed and filed, and consequently he lost his possessions.

It was a sad blow for the old hero, but he bore up bravely, as he did under all his afflictions. When he found that he must lose his home and land, he decided to begin anew west of the Mississippi.

"Are you going into the wilderness again?" asked his wife.

"Yes, I want more elbow room. They are getting

settled up too thick about me. I want to go back into the forest, where I can once more hunt the buffalo and deer."

"But you are getting too old," she argued.

"Too old? bah! My arm is as steady and my eye as true as ever. I'll bring down the game at every shot, never fear."

"But there is another reason. The country west of the Mississippi is owned by Spain. Would you give up an English home for a Spanish one?"

"Our home is where we make it, Rebecca," he answered. "We can be good Spanish subjects, as well as good Americans."

Daniel Boone, having spent most of his life on the frontier, neither knew nor cared much about political affairs.

Another reason for his deciding to go into Upper Louisiana, or Missouri, was an invitation from Delassus, who later became the Spanish lieutenant governor, and who well knew the worth of such a man as Daniel Boone in building up a new country. Delassus was a wise, patriotic, and unambitious man. He saw that there was a great future for the country over which he afterward held control, but he knew that its resources could not be developed unless it was first peopled. The Anglo-Saxon race had been pouring into the valleys of the Ohio and the Cumberland from the Atlantic States. If these emigrants could be induced to come west of the Mississippi, the territory might be filled up with a desirable class of inhabitants. No man on the frontier was more highly respected and better able to help in this work than Daniel Boone, and hence Delassus was anxious to have him move into Upper Louisiana.

About the year 1797, the old pioneer went over into Missouri and settled in what was known as the Femme Osage (Osage Woman) settlement. This was on the Missouri River in the district of St. Charles, about forty-five miles west of St. Louis, and about twenty-five miles above the town of St. Charles. This portion of Missouri was then wild and picturesque, — just such a country as he loved. Here in the deep forest, where no woodman's ax had yet been heard, he built him a log cabin home.

He was now too old to join in the exciting chase, as he had done in his youth, but with his trusty rifle he would often stroll to the haunts of the deer and elk. Here on the bank of some stream he would quietly lie, sure of his game when the animals came to drink.

Soon after his arrival in Missouri, Daniel Boone renounced his allegiance to the government of the United States, and became a Spanish subject. On June 11, 1800, Delassus appointed him commandant, or syndic, of the Femme Osage district, a position which he accepted. The office was both civil and military. In time of peace, he acted as an adjudicator, or judge, over the people in his district, and in time of war he was their commander.

The matters on which he had to pass judgment were such as required honesty and practical common sense, rather than a knowledge of law. He was fearless and upright in his decisions. On one occasion, a desperado who had been terrorizing the people of the Femme Osage district was publicly reprimanded by Boone. The man, who prided himself on his power to overawe the people, cried out, —

"If you were not an old man, I should not take that from you."

"You great coward," responded Boone, shaking his clenched fist close to the man's face, "if you want to get revenge on me for what I said, don't let my gray hairs stand in the way. Old as I am, I am young enough to whip you." Quite crestfallen, the fellow slunk away and was never again heard to say anything against the old pioneer.

There is a story told of one of Boone's decisions, which shows his kindness of heart, as well as his scrupulous honesty. There lived in his settlement a grasping, miserly fellow who had emigrated to Missouri from Virginia. This man had a claim against a widow who was very poor.

The claim was no doubt a lawful one, but Boone thought that under the circumstances the man ought not to have pressed it. The widow had but one cow, and this the claimant had seized to satisfy his debt. When the commandant had heard the testimony on both sides, he said, —

"The widow owes you, Tom Turley; yet you are a scoundrel to take her only cow to pay the debt. The law says you shall have it. Take it and go, but never look an honest man in the face again."

Then, turning to the widow, he added, "Let him have it; I'll give you a better one."

He kept his word, for that very day his sons drove a fine cow to the home of the widow.

Though acting as a sort of judge, Boone's ignorance of law made him once more a victim of legal technicalities. The Spanish lieutenant governor, Delassus, had in the first place given him a grant of a thousand arpents (about 980 acres) of land in the Femme Osage district; and he afterwards received a further grant of ten thousand arpents, for bringing into Upper Louisiana one hundred families from Virginia and Kentucky. The latter transaction was the result of a definite contract; and the people whom Boone induced to immigrate into Missouri represented some of the best families of the frontier.

Now, in order to confirm the grants, it was necessary to obtain the signature of the direct representative of the Spanish crown, who at that time resided in the city of New Orleans. As Boone neglected to comply with this requirement, his titles to both tracts of land were declared invalid; but after the country became part of the United States his first grant was confirmed by an act of Congress. This saved to him only a part of what was justly his own.

When all Louisiana was purchased by the United States, Boone and his sons again became American citizens. Though the old pioneer was well advanced in years, he took a lively interest in the affairs of the country. He even participated in some of the early struggles with the Indians in Missouri.

The red men feared him, even when his eye had grown dim, and his hand feeble with age. It is said that a Sac chief was once leading his warriors to attack a fort held by the whites, when he learned that Daniel Boone was in the fort. He at once stopped his men, turned them about, and started back to his own village, saying, "It is no use to fight if he is in the fort."

On March 18, 1813, the brave pioneer's wife died. She was buried on the top of a beautiful hill overlooking the Missouri River, about one mile southeast of the town of Marthasville, in Warren County. Daniel Boone was never the same cheerful, happy old man after her death.

On September 26, 1820, Boone himself died, at the residence of his son, Major Nathan Boone, on Femme Osage Creek, in St. Charles County. He was eighty-eight years of age. The house in which he died is still standing. It is of stone, and was the first of the kind ever built in the State.

Daniel Boone was buried by the side of his wife, in a cherry coffin which he had made himself, and had kept ready for several years. In 1845, both he and his wife were disinterred and their bodies taken to Frankfort, Kentucky, where they were buried with all the honors and ceremonies due to a hero.

IX.

MATURIN BOUVET AND THE OSAGES.

DURING the administration of Delassus, there was a constant immigration into the villages and settlements of Upper Louisiana. Not only were a number of settlers induced to move from the United States to Missouri, but a great many French people came up from New Orleans and what is now Louisiana.

This immigration was attended by a frenzied spirit of speculation. Every one was seeking land, which was then given by grant, and not by deed as at present. These grants required long legal proceedings to make them valid, and have been the cause of much litigation in the courts.

It was not a healthy speculation. The men did not intend to improve the land, but simply wanted to hold it until it increased in value and could be sold at great profit. In some cases a large tract would be secured by a single person. A man in St. Charles, named James Mackay, obtained a grant for thirty thousand acres; and Francis Sevier received one for eight thousand eight hundred acres.

We can hardly understand at this day why such large grants should have been made; we must remember, however, that from the Mississippi to New Mexico the country was one vast wilderness. For this reason, a thousand acres seemed to be no more, comparatively, than a grain of sand on the ocean beach. To fix the exact location of the many grants made, surveys were extended a long distance in every direction, although the men engaged in them were liable to be attacked by roving bands of Indians.

At this time there lived in St. Charles a Frenchman named Maturin Bouvet. He was a noted hunter and Indian trader. From one of the young men who had been some distance into the upper country, he learned that there was a salt spring in the forest, and he went to investigate it for himself. He found the water so briny that he determined to bring kettles and manufacture salt from it.

The Indians had shown a spirit of unfriendliness for several months, and Bouvet was warned not to venture so far from the settlements; but he was a daring man, and paid no heed to his advisers. With his kettles and a few companions, he embarked upon the river and drifted down to the mouth of the Missouri. Then he sailed up the Mississippi, and continued on till he reached the stream on which the salt spring had been discovered. This is supposed to have been one of the tributaries of Salt River, in either Pike or Ralls County.

When the spring was reached, the men cut some poles with their axes, and from them made a rude shanty. Its shelter was hardly sufficient to protect them from the storms.

The country about them was wild, with no human inhabitant near, unless the wandering bands of Indians could be called inhabitants. At night the wild animals came so near to the camp that the men could see the fire light reflected in their eyes. One day a party of Indians came, but the white men drove them away.

When they had finished their shanty, they built a furnace and hung over it their kettles, which they filled with water from the salt spring. Then they boiled the water until it had all evaporated, and nothing but the salt remained. The yield was considerable.

One day, while the salt makers were away from the camp chasing a wounded deer, some Indians came to it and stole three blankets and a few other articles.

On discovering his loss, Bouvet was furious. With his companions, he pursued the thieves far into the woods and across the prairies, but did not overtake them. He then went to Delassus, represented that he had been robbed, and demanded reparation. The lieutenant governor, always generous in making land grants, gave him "twenty arpents square" for the trifling loss he had sustained. On the same day, by the way, Delassus made two large grants for distillery purposes, and a third to supply the fuel necessary for their use; and the first distillery in St. Louis was built by Auguste Chouteau, who received one of these grants.

The "twenty arpents square" granted to Maturin Bouvet were west of Ste. Genevieve. He engaged four assistants to help him survey his land. Hostile Osages were in the vicinity, and Bouvet was warned to defer locating the bounds; but, as daring as he was avaricious, he said, —

"I'm not afraid of them. They won't come within reach of our rifles."

With his four companions, and all the implements necessary to a surveying party, he started out into the forest. To protect themselves from the Indians, the white men carried rifles slung over their shoulders, even when at work. One day, while running a line across a strip of prairie, one of Bouvet's companions looked over a small stream, and said, —

"There they are!"

"Indians!" exclaimed Bouvet.

A party of a dozen savages could be seen standing on a slight elevation, just across the stream. They were gazing coolly at the white men, whom they evidently regarded as intruders. Bouvet and his companions dropped their surveying implements, and grasped their rifles. The Indians, however, showed no inclination to attack them, and after a few moments went away into the forest.

"There! they are gone," said Bouvet. "We shan't see any more of them."

"Don't be deceived; they'll get reinforcements and come back," said one of his companions.

"Nonsense! they'll never bother us," declared Bouvet.

No doubt the Frenchman had his land grant in mind, and feared that the Indians would frighten his men away. With the above remark the subject was dropped, and the men resumed their work.

Next morning, while they were still around their camp, preparing breakfast, they heard what sounded like a turkey in the woods. One of the men, a Kentuckian named Lewis, seized his gun, and started into the dense wood, saying, —

"I'll be back soon with a fat gobbler."

The noise he heard was not made by a turkey, but by an Indian. By using a bone taken from a turkey's wing, the savages could produce a sound so like the real call as to deceive a wild turkey itself. Such a bone was often used by hunters as a decoy, and was known as a "turkey call" or "cowker."

Lewis had been absent but a few moments when those in the camp heard the report of a gun.

"There, he's got one of them," said one of the surveyors.

Two more reports in quick succession puzzled and alarmed them. They had just seized their guns, when Lewis ran through the camp, his left arm shattered by a bullet.

"Indians! Indians!" he shouted.

Bouvet tried to induce his men to make a stand, but they fled without firing a shot. The Indians, a party of Osages, came hurrying toward the camp; and Bouvet shot the first one that came in sight. This caused the others to halt. The Frenchman took advantage of the delay to reload his gun, and then, seeing that there were more than a score of the Osages, he decided to escape if he could.

A few rods to his left was a ravine, and toward this he ran. The Indians, discovering his design, fired several shots at him. One of their balls wounded him in the left leg, but he limped to the ravine and jumped in. The bed was dry, stony, and covered with leaves.

The Osages, seeing they had but one man to deal with, became bolder and pressed forward. They knew that the white man was wounded, and counted his capture as sure. They opened fire on him. The bullets whistled about his ears; they cut off the twigs and leaves of the trees that grew along the sides of the ravine, and shattered the bark from the bodies of the saplings, but did not touch Bouvet.

At last he turned and fired at the savages, wounding one of them. The Indians, knowing that his gun was empty, then ran down the hill and threw themselves upon him. He made a desperate fight for his life, keeping them off for a while with the butt of his rifle and with his knife; but before long he was knocked down with a club, and made captive. He was taken to the Osage village, where he was subjected to the most horrible tortures, and finally burned at the stake.

It was many years before his fate was known; but at last one of the Indians who was present told how he was captured and put to death.

This was but one of the many incidents of the kind which happened to those who surveyed the land grants of Delassus. And this was not the only trouble which those grants were destined to cause. Owing to defective proof of transfer, indefinite description of the local boundaries, and sometimes doubtful or insufficient evidence of actual occupancy, they were fruitful of long and expensive lawsuits, lasting years after Missouri became a State.

X.

LOUISIANA PURCHASE.

GLANCING carelessly at history, one might think that the conduct of France and Spain over Louisiana was not unlike that of two children with a plaything. France was the big child, and Spain the smaller one. In a seeming fit of good humor, France, as has been stated, gave Louisiana to Spain in 1762. Then, after Spain had had possession for a time, France wanted it back, and, being the "biggest," got it: the date of this cession was October 1, 1800.

All this seems at first like child's play; and, when we consider the secrecy with which the transfers were made, it is a little mysterious. But there was a deep meaning behind it all. There were sound reasons for each step, and the transfers are of importance in the history of Europe as well as in that of Missouri.

During the latter part of the eighteenth century and first part of the nineteenth, France and England were bitter enemies. One might be justified in suspecting that the generosity of France to Spain in 1762 was from a fear that the British government would seize Louisiana. The beginning of the nineteenth century showed a different state of affairs. England had lost almost all her possessions in America except Canada, and some statesmen thought that France would now be able to hold Louisiana.

Napoleon, the great general of whom we read so much, was at this time engaged in a terrible war with nearly all Europe. Successful as he had been, there were some who doubted that he could continue to be so. England was an enemy that Napoleon had not been able to injure. For political reasons, many doubted the wisdom of getting back the Louisiana territory; but Napoleon insisted, and in 1800 the treaty was signed which put it once more under French control.

Scarcely, however, had France come into possession of it, when Napoleon began to fear that the British would take it from him. It was too far away for him to protect, especially while England remained the strongest power on the seas. For this reason, the retrocession of Louisiana, as it was called, was kept a secret for some time. Indeed, France never formally took possession of the territory until after she had sold it to the United States.

The United States government, through its minister, Robert R. Livingston, had for some time been trying to gain possession of a part of this valuable country. The French had once been compelled to part with Louisiana to prevent the British from getting it, and Napoleon finally concluded that they had better do so again. The United States had successfully resisted Great Britain, and, after a seven years' war, had gained independence. Between the two great English-speaking countries there was at that time no real friendship, though they were at peace. Napoleon knew of no better purchaser than the United States, and the sale was made. The treaty was signed in Paris, April 30, 1803, during the first administration of Thomas Jefferson.

"To-day I have given to England a maritime rival that will sooner or later humble her pride," said Napoleon, after he had signed the contract which gave all Louisiana to the United States.

"We have lived long, but this is the noblest work of our whole lives," said Livingston to Marbois, the French representative. "The treaty which we have just signed will change vast solitudes into flourishing districts. From this day the United States take their place among the powers of the first rank."

It was a great transaction; an affair of mighty consequence to Missouri and the whole United States. By it our government acquired a vast domain, extending from the Gulf of Mexico to the British possessions on the north, and from the Mississippi River to the Rocky Mountains; for Louisiana then comprised all the present States of Louisiana, Arkansas, Missouri, Iowa, Nebraska, South and North Dakota, and Montana; Indian Territory; and parts of Minnesota, Wyoming, Colorado, Kansas, and Oklahoma.

The price paid France was sixty million francs, equal to almost twelve million dollars. In addition, the United States agreed to assume certain claims which citizens of this country had against France, amounting to three millions. This made the territory cost, altogether, fifteen millions of dollars, or less than three cents an acre.

Some declared that the President had no authority

to make the purchase. President Jefferson admitted that he stretched his power "till it cracked"; but though he doubted his own authority, he did not doubt the wisdom of the transaction. In giving his reasons for making the purchase, he said, —

"There is on the globe one single spot, the possessor of which is our natural and habitual enemy. It is New Orleans, through which the produce of three eighths of our territory must pass to market. This territory, from its fertility, will yield more than half of our whole produce, and contain more than half of our inhabitants."

Though many opposed the measure of Jefferson, a majority agreed with him in the wisdom of his policy. The Louisiana purchase prevented Great Britain from seizing the territory, extinguished the French claim, and made it impossible for any other monarchy to gain a new foothold in North America. Had it not been made, it is possible that Missouri would to-day be subject to some foreign power.

As already stated, the purchase was made in 1803; in October of the same year, the treaty was ratified by the United States Senate.

On December 20, the American troops entered the city of New Orleans. Nine days later, at midday, the flag of France which floated from the staff in the public square of New Orleans began to descend. At the same time, the stars and stripes of the American Union appeared above the crowd, and slowly mounted the pole. Midway, the two flags met. Then amidst the thunders of cannon, the music of "Hail Columbia," the cheers of spectators, and the waving of handkerchiefs and banners, the tricolor continued its descent to the ground, and the flag of the United States soared rapidly aloft and flung out its folds to the breeze on the summit of the staff.

Though Louisiana proper was surrendered to the United States December 29, 1803, it was not until March 9, 1804, that Upper Louisiana was formally handed over to the American authorities. On that day, the American troops crossed the river from Cahokia, Illinois, and Don Carlos Delassus delivered the territory to Captain Amos Stoddard of the United States army.

A little explanation may make clear a point which seems somewhat confused. Upper Louisiana had not up to this time been surrendered to France. Delassus, the lieutenant governor, still ruled the country as a Spanish official. In order to make the transfer regular and legal, Captain Stoddard was made the agent of France, to receive from Spain the formal surrender of Upper Louisiana. This took place March 9, 1804, and on the next day the territory was transferred from France to the United States, according to the treaty.

On March 8, 1804, Missouri belonged to Spain, on the 9th it belonged to France, and on the 10th it was the property of the United States. In three days, Upper Louisiana belonged to three different nations.

Though the people of St. Louis were in sympathy with the new republic in the east, they were strongly attached to the old government. It was with feelings of regret and apprehension that they saw the stars and stripes take the place of the well-known flag of Spain.

The transfer worked a wonderful change in St. Louis and all the other Missouri settlements. Business became more brisk, and the population was rapidly increased by an energetic and thrifty class of settlers, who came from the eastern and southern States.

On March 26, 1804, two weeks after Captain Stoddard assumed command of St. Louis, Congress passed an act dividing Louisiana into two parts. The southern part was known as the Territory of Orleans, and later became the State of Louisiana. The northern part was at first called the District of Louisiana, and was attached, for administrative purposes, to Indiana Territory. The next year, however, it was itself made a Territory, and General Wilkinson of the United States army was appointed the first governor.

The capital of the Territory was St. Louis, and the executive offices were in the old government building on Main Street, just south of the public square, called La Place d'Armes.

XI.

THE FIRST SCHOOLMASTERS.

AN action often produces a result entirely different from that which was expected or planned. What is intended as an injury to a person or country sometimes results in a benefit.

When Aaron Burr, in 1805, conspired to seize all the western Territories and States, annex them to Mexico, and set up an empire, he hoped not only to make himself the emperor, but also to strike a blow at the United States government, which he hated. His effort resulted in his own ruin, but was of some practical benefit to Missouri.

In 1805 Burr went to St. Louis and held an interview with General Wilkinson, then governor of the Territory. His object was to induce the general to join him in his enterprise of setting up a new empire. Some of Burr's friends insist that Governor Wilkinson did consent to aid in the conspiracy, but they are of doubtful authority, and Wilkinson himself always denied having any such intentions.

Burr organized his expedition, started down the Ohio with a fleet of keel boats, and entered the Mississippi with a number of armed men. They were arrested by the United States authorities, and Burr was taken a prisoner to Virginia, where he was tried and acquitted. The most of Burr's followers were confined in Missouri, where, after a few weeks or months of imprisonment, they also were acquitted. Many of them were young men from New York City, who were naturally not at all fitted for the rugged life of pioneers. They were men of education and refinement, who now found themselves thrown into a most unfortunate position, with no means of getting back to their far-off homes on the Atlantic coast.

Their situation was really deplorable. Left as they were without money, hundreds of miles away from home, surrounded by people with ways and manners wholly different from their own, and yet compelled to live with them, it became a serious question how the young strangers should earn their livelihood. They could not cut down the great trees, nor plow the prairies, nor hunt and trap, as did the hardy frontiersmen.

Of what avail was all education in this wilderness, where muscle, and not brains, was in demand? At last one of them suggested that they turn teachers. They decided to do so; and, according to the statement of an official of the time, they supplied the Territory with dancing masters, writing masters, and school-teachers for many years.

A band of these itinerant pedagogues went up the river to St. Louis and spread over Missouri, pursuing their vocation. They were the first professional school-teachers Missouri ever had. Their lot was a hard one, but they planted the seeds of education, and did much good. Except what little the priests had been able to do in mission schools, education was unknown in Missouri until Burr's expedition supplied the Territory with teachers.

The country was thinly populated, and the people poor. There were no schoolhouses outside of three or four towns, and the first schools were taught in the cabins of the people. Sometimes a night school was added, which the parents attended.

Spelling, reading, writing, and arithmetic were the only branches thought essential at that time. The schoolmaster was paid so much "a head," or for each scholar. He lived with the people in the neighborhood where he taught, and assisted in making fires, splitting wood, milking cows, and in other odd jobs to earn his board.

He was paid whatever the people could afford to give him. The great hope of these teachers was to accumulate enough money to return to their homes across the Alleghanies; but year after year passed by, and they were still as poor as when they were freed from prison. Few, if any, ever returned to New York.

Congress appropriated the common fields of the villages to school purposes, but it was a long time before Missouri derived any benefit from a public school fund. There was nothing of the kind during the time of Burr's teachers.

When these first itinerant pedagogues, or wandering schoolmasters, became tired of teaching in private houses, they urged the people in the settlements to erect separate buildings for school purposes. In one neighborhood, the frontiersmen began to discuss the plan, and a majority of them approved of it.

Ste. Genevieve, St. Louis, and St. Charles already had cabins which were used for schoolhouses; and these men thought that there was no reason why other settlements should not have them also.

One day the settlers gathered at a spot agreed upon, with their axes in their hands, for the purpose of beginning their first schoolhouse. The schoolmaster came with them to superintend the affair.

They began to cut down trees, hew the sides, and notch the ends. Then they laid log upon log until the walls were of the right height. A door was sawed out of one side, and a log left out on the opposite side for the window. Nearly a whole end was taken up with a huge fireplace, above which rose a stick-and-mud chimney. The cracks between the logs were chinked and daubed with clay, mixed with leaves and grass.

Some of the men split thin slabs from logs and hewed one side smooth. These were the puncheons of which the floor was made. In other cabin schoolhouses there was often no floor at all. The furniture was composed of benches without backs, and a long thin slab or board for a writing desk. The long window was without glass, but a thin piece of cloth or paper was pasted over it to keep out the wind in winter. In houses of this sort were taught the first schools in Missouri.

What text-books did they use? Almost anything. The only regularity was in the spelling book and arithmetic. For readers some had the New Testament, others Bunyan's "Pilgrim's Progress," Weem's "Life of Marion," of Washington, or of Franklin, or any other book that the family had, or could borrow.

St. Louis, St. Charles, Boone, and Howard counties were the first to enjoy anything like respectable schools. As new counties were laid out and settled, each had to pass through the stage of the log schoolhouse, with three months' schooling a year, and the teacher boarding about among the scholars.

Before there was a county school fund, or a county commissioner, the trustees often took it upon themselves to examine an applicant as to his qualifications. The teachers in those days were usually ignorant, and their examiners more so.

There is a story told of one of these examinations, which illustrates the ignorance of both teacher and trustees. The applicant was asked if the earth was round or flat. He answered that he wasn't quite sure, but that he was prepared to teach it either way. After a conference on the part of the trustees, it was decided that he should teach that it was flat.

The school children in those days were mischievous,

much as they are now in country districts. They had a fashion of "turning the master out" on the last day of school, or at the beginning of the holidays, to make him treat. They would go to the schoolhouse before he did, and bar the door so that he could not get in. It was their purpose to keep him out until he would agree to give them a treat of apples or candy.

Sometimes the teacher took this joke all in good part, and sometimes he did not. If he was too obstinate, the "big boys" would seize him and carry him to the nearest stream or pond, and "duck him" in the water until he would agree to treat. Often they would have to cut the ice before they could dip him under the water.

XII.

EARLY MISSOURIANS.

WHEN Louisiana was purchased by the United States, St. Louis was only a village, laid out and built according to the French plan. There were two long streets running parallel with the river, and a number of others intersecting them at right angles.

A few houses stood on a line with what is now Third Street, then known as *La rue des Granges*, or "The Street of Barns." The church building on Second Street was an ordinary "hewed log house." West of Fourth Street, there was little else than woods and commons. The largest house in St. Louis was the government building on Main Street, near Walnut.

There was no post office, and no need of one, for there was no regular postal service in Missouri. A village merchant, however, would bring letters home with his goods, and stick them up in the windows of his store, so that the owners could come and get them. He also took it upon himself to forward letters for his customers.

Government boats occasionally ran between St. Louis and New Orleans, but there was no regular passenger or freight line. Furs and lead were the principal articles of export, for farming had hardly become an industry. Corn, wheat, and vegetables were grown, but only in sufficient quantity to supply home demands.

Le Clerc, who lived on Main Street, between Walnut and Elm, was the only baker in the town; and as yet there were but three blacksmiths and only one physician. There were two little French taverns, both near the corner of Main and Locust streets. One was kept by Yostic, and the other by Laudreville.

Merchants were numerous, but they held their goods at very high prices. A store at that time was quite different from one of to-day. A place only a few feet square would contain the entire stock of a merchant. Indeed, it was not unusual for one of the first traders in town to keep his goods in a box or chest, supplied with a lid, which he opened when he wished to display his wares to a customer.

Soon after St. Louis became an American town, a post office was found to be necessary. Immigrants were pouring into the new Territory, and St. Louis and the adjoining settlements were increasing their population. The newcomers had friends in the South and East with whom they wished to correspond, and the business of the town had made it more important than many a place of its size. In 1804 the first official post office in St. Louis was established, with Mr. Rufus Easton as postmaster.

Mr. Joseph Charless came to St. Louis soon after Louisiana became the property of the United States. He was a printer by trade, and had a contract to do the printing for the Territory. Mr. Charless was an intelligent, enterprising gentleman, and he foresaw a great future for the new town. He conceived the idea of establishing a newspaper in St. Louis, although none as yet had ever been published west of the Mississippi.

When Charless mentioned the matter to some friends, they advised against the enterprise; but he was not to be deterred from his purpose, and on July 12, 1808, he issued the first number of the *Missouri Gazette*. It was a sheet no larger than a royal octavo page. Notwithstanding the many predictions of failure, the *Missouri Gazette* prospered, and after the first few months became self-sustaining. The name was afterward changed to the *Missouri Republican*, and still later it became the *St. Louis Republic*, which is now one of the large daily papers of the city.

On November 9, 1809, St. Louis was incorporated as a town, upon the petition of the taxpayers, under the authority of an act of the Territory of Louisiana passed the year before.

As is usually the case on the frontier, Missouri was for some time the abode of rough and lawless men; but among them were to be found those who were quiet and honorable. In fact, some who were called lawless were honest enough in their own way. They might not hesitate to end a quarrel in bloodshed, yet at the same time would not swindle a man out of a cent. Courts were held irregularly in the different districts into which the Territory had been divided. Real estate had increased in value, and the claim jumper, squatter, and land pirate had already appeared on the scene. The pistol and knife were often resorted to in the settlement of disputed claims.

Much has been said about the rough character of the early Missourians. Some of it is false, and yet a great deal is true. The frontiersman learned to depend on his rifle to supply him with food and to protect his home. Constantly coming in contact with rude men, he partook of their nature. Liable at any time to be shot or stabbed, he learned to shoot and stab on his own account.

Though a frontiersman might be ever so agreeable and pleasant a companion, he was a dangerous person to quarrel with. Lawsuits and disputes over conflicting claims or mining rights often led to bloody contests.

There lived in St. Louis about the year 1809 two men, known as Colonel S. and Mr. P. They were the best of friends. Both were gentlemen, as Dickens says, of the "good old stock"; that is, if we take the stock of a century ago to be good.

They had known each other for years, and had never quarreled. But at last they got into a dispute over a mining claim located in the Ste. Genevieve district. Colonel S. pondered long over the matter, and at last made up his mind that there was but one course to pursue. He called one day on his neighbor, and, finding him alone, said in his coolest manner, "Good morning, Mr. P."

"Good morning, Colonel S. Pray be seated." And the man handed his friend a chair.

The colonel seated himself, and a serious expression came over his face as he said, "Mr. P., we have been friends for a long time —"

"Yes, Colonel," interrupted Mr. P., quietly. "We have long been friends."

"And I feel a great regret that any misunderstanding should have arisen between us," resumed the colonel, wiping his troubled face with his handkerchief.

"So do I, Colonel, I greatly regret it," put in Mr. P.

"Here we are entirely alone, and there is no one to interrupt us. Let us settle the matter in an amicable way."

"Certainly, certainly," assented Mr. P., before whose vision there arose a plan of peaceful adjustment of their difficulties.

"You know my aversion to lawyers and their quibbles," continued the colonel. "I have here a couple of friends that have no mistake in them." Hereupon he drew a brace of pistols and presented their butts to his friend. "Take your choice; they are both loaded and equally true."

Mr. P. drew back and thanked him kindly, but declined the offer.

"Why, my dear Colonel, I would rather lose the whole claim than harm a hair of your head," he said.

"So would I. Let us divide, arbitrate, or anything you wish."

Their dispute was satisfactorily settled, and bloodshed was averted.

Dueling was confined to what were called gentlemen of note, politicians, and leaders in society. It was at this period common in the East as well as the West. The man who had fought a duel, though he might be a murderer, was a sort of hero. In some instances these duelers have been elevated to the highest positions of honor and trust. There was some excuse for this state of affairs in Missouri. That part of the country still felt the effect of French influence, and with the French nation dueling has not even yet gone out of fashion.

Mr. Timothy Flint, a New England clergyman, writes the following about the people of Louisiana at this time; — and by Louisiana he meant what is now Missouri, —

"It is true there are many worthless people here, and the most worthless, it must be confessed, are from New England. It is true there are gamblers, and gougers, and outlaws; but there are fewer of them than from the nature of things and the character of the age and the world, we ought to expect. I have traveled in these regions thousands of miles, under all circumstances of exposure and danger, and this too in many instances where I was not known to be a minister, or where such knowledge would have had no influence in protecting me. I have never carried the slightest weapon of defense."

Mr. Flint is regarded by all historians as the most impartial writer concerning the people of Louisiana at that early day. His travels extended over nearly all the Mississippi valley, and his book is said to be the best description of the people west of the Mississippi that has ever been published. Mr. Flint draws a fine picture of the backwoodsman of the time: —

"He is generally an amiable and virtuous man. He has vices and barbarisms peculiar to his situation. His manners are rough. He wears, it may be, a long beard. He has a great quantity of bear or deer skin wrought into his household establishment, his furniture, and dress. He carries a knife or dirk in his bosom, and when in the woods has his rifle at his back and a pack of dogs at his heels. An Atlantic stranger transferred directly from one of our cities to his door would recoil from the encounter with him. But remember that his gun and his dogs are among his chief means of support and profit. Remember that all his first days here were passed in dread of savages. Remember that he still encounters them, still meets bears and panthers. Enter his door and tell him you are benighted, and wish the shelter of his cabin for the night. The welcome is indeed seemingly ungracious, —

"'I reckon you can stay,' or 'I suppose we must let you stay.' But this apparent ungraciousness is the harbinger of every kindness he can bestow, and every comfort his cabin can afford. Good coffee, corn bread and butter, venison, pork, wild and tame fowls, are set before you. His wife, timid, silent, reserved, but constantly attentive to your comfort, does not sit at the table with you, but like the wives of the patriarchs stands and attends on you. You are shown the best bed the house can offer. When the kind hospitality has been afforded you as long as you choose to stay, and when you depart, and speak of your bill, you are most commonly told, with some slight mark of resentment, that they 'don't keep tavern.' Even the flaxen-haired children will turn away from your money.

"If we were to try them by the standard of New England customs and opinions, that is to say, the customs of a people under entirely different circumstances, there would be things in the picture that would strike us offensively. They care little about ministers, and less about paying them. They are averse to all and even the most necessary restraints. They are destitute of the forms and observances of society and religion; but they are sincere and kind without professions, and have a coarse but substantial morality."

Occasionally in the older counties of Missouri may still be seen one of the quaint little cabins of these early pioneers. It is half house and half fortress. A few years ago some of the old French houses, plastered within and without, were still standing in St. Louis and St. Charles counties. Some may even yet be found, a monument of a bygone people who laid the corner stone of this great commonwealth.

XIII.

WESTERN BOATMEN.

UNDER the treaty between Great Britain and France, and still later between Great Britain and Spain, these three nations were to have free use of the Mississippi River. English boats floated down the Ohio into the Mississippi, and thence to New Orleans. From St. Louis, the Spanish and French boats joined the English, and often a dozen of the barks called keel boats would glide down the great stream together. When the thirteen colonies gained their independence, England ceded her rights over the river to the new nation.

At the time of the Louisiana purchase, a class of hardy frontiersmen, known as "boatmen," had sprung into existence. These were men who earned their living by working on the boats which ran up and down the western rivers; for now it was no longer the custom for each settler to take his own produce to market. The boatmen were brave and muscular, but rude and uneducated; their lives were full of toil and stirring adventure.

Conspicuous among these early navigators was an Irish-American named Mike Fink. He was born in Pittsburg, and we first hear of him as a boatman on the Ohio, where he became famous both at the oar and with his rifle. He was made the hero of an early romance, and songs were sung in his praise.

According to his biographer, he was "strong as an ox, and brave as a lion." He was said to be the best marksman in the West; and at all the shooting matches he was ruled out on account of his skill. Though the novelist and poet have tried to cast a halo of romance about Mike, he was, like many other heroes, only a cruel, treacherous bully.

His keel boat was called the "Light-foot," and as it glided down the river Fink used to amuse himself by shooting the tails off from pigs on the shore, without doing them any other harm. He had a friend named Carpenter, who was almost as fine a marksman as himself. The two used to entertain their companions by shooting tin cups off each other's head.

Once, while on a trip up the Mississippi River, Mike and his friend quarreled, but "made up"; and then, to prove their friendship, they decided to indulge in the tin cup amusement. They drew lots to see which should have the first shot, and the lot fell to Mike. He fired, and Carpenter fell dead. Mike claimed at first that it was an accident, and among the boatmen in the wilderness it passed as such. But a few months later he declared that he had killed Carpenter on purpose, and was glad of it. A man named Talbot, who was a friend of Carpenter, heard Fink's boast, and shot him dead on the spot.

There were, however, very few such boatmen as Mike Fink. He gained a reputation for cruelty by which he is remembered to this day.

The keel boats of this time were similar to those of the earliest settlers. They were propelled by the current, aided by sweeps, when going down the stream, but were usually "cordelled" upstream, though sails were sometimes used. Such was the first mode of navigation to and from Missouri; and for many years all transportation of freight was done either in this way, or by means of pack horses.

There were two methods of cordelling a boat up the stream. Sometimes one end of a long rope was carried on ahead and fastened to some object in the river or on shore, and the crew then stood in the bow and propelled the boat by pulling on the rope. The usual method, however, was for the crew to walk along the shore and pull the boat after them as canal mules do.

There is an amusing story told of an Irishman working his passage up the Mississippi in a keel boat. He was at Ste. Genevieve, and wanted to go to St. Louis. Learning that a boat was going up the river to that place, he asked the captain if he might work his passage.

"Certainly," said the captain, who stood in the bow of the boat with a long pole in his hand.

The Irishman took his carpetbag aboard. When all were ready to start, he joined the crew on shore, and, seizing the rope, assisted in pulling the craft upstream. After two or three miles of such navigation he said,—

"Faith, if it wasn't for the name of riding, I'd about as soon walk."

Keel boats were large in those days. They had cabins, and carried passengers as well as freight. Men, women, and children often took voyages on the rivers in these rude boats.

A man who started down the Mississippi in a keel boat, which was wrecked above New Madrid, has left an account of the disaster. This gentleman had under his charge a cousin, who was going to join her husband in New Orleans.

"One dark, rainy night our boat drifted rapidly downstream with the current. We usually 'tied up along the shore' on very dark nights, but our captain, who was also pilot, declared he could steer in the darkest night that ever came.

"Most of the passengers had retired to their cabins and were asleep, when suddenly there came a crash which sent me out of my berth on to the floor. I sprang to my feet, and my first thought was of Nancy (the lady under my charge). I ran to her cabin and found her up and dressed, and not nearly so badly frightened as I had feared she would be.

"'What has happened?' she asked.

"'The boat has struck a snag, and may sink. Stay right here until I come for you.'

"Then I went on deck, where all was confusion. There were twelve or fifteen passengers there, running about like mad people.

"The most excited of all were five men from St. Louis. They had dragged their trunks and carpet-bags to the deck, and were calling for a skiff or yawl to take them ashore. All the captain and mate could do or say to quiet them was in vain. Three or four lanterns were lighted, and served to increase the terror of all by revealing the black, turbid waters into which we were sinking.

"The men who had brought their trunks on deck seized one of the yawls, leaped in with their baggage, before any one could prevent them, and pulled to shore, which the flashes of lightning showed was not more than thirty yards away.

"About the time they landed with their baggage, I observed that the boat began to rock just like a basin sinking in shallow water. The captain noticed this also, and shouted,—

"'You are all safe. The boat is on a sand bar, and can't sink.'

"In fact, one of the crew had cast the lead line a moment before, and had discovered that we were in only about five feet of water. In a moment our keel settled on the sand bar, with the deck and cabins two feet above water. I went back to Nancy, who was anxiously awaiting my return.

"'What shall we do?' she asked.

"'Go to bed and sleep until morning,' I answered.

"She did so. It rained all night. It was one of those cold, disagreeable rains that make one shiver, and one's bones ache. Next morning we saw five or six wet, miserable wretches sitting on the bank, shivering, and begging the captain to take them on board.

"They were the selfish cowards who would have escaped with their luggage and left the remainder of us to drown. Their haste to get on land was so great that they forgot to moor the yawl in which they went ashore, and it had floated away.

"Though the captain had another, he would not send for them, and left them all night in the rain. But soon after daylight he sent and brought them all on board.

"Our boat had struck a snag which knocked a hole in the bottom; but fortunately, after striking, we came immediately to such shallow water that we could not sink.

"We lived in this grounded boat for over a week before another keel boat came and took us down the river to our journey's end."

The dangers of wind and wave were not all that the daring boatmen had to encounter. The wild shores were inhabited by hostile savages, who often attacked them.

"Many a time I have helped cordelle a boat upstream, expecting every moment to be shot down by an ambushed savage," said an old keel-boatman. "Often I have seen the man before me drop by a shot fired from the bushes, and have felt the wind of the Indians' bullets on my face.

"Once, as we were cordelling our boat up the Missouri, the captain had just called out, 'Hand over hand,' which means to take up the slack on the rope, and pull closer to shore. Just then there came the crack of a gun from the bushes up the bank, and Joe Fugate, next before me, went down.

"'All aboard!' shouted the captain; and he shoved the bow in to within six feet of shore. By this time the Indians' bullets from the hill were whistling like hail about us. Two of the boys carried Joe to the boat, and we all got on. Joe was laid in a comfortable place, for he was badly hurt, and the rest of us ran for our guns, while the boat was pushed out into the current.

"We always carried our guns strapped on our backs when we thought there was danger; but this attack was a complete surprise. Seizing my rifle, I fired at an Indian who was running down the steep bank toward us, and missed. Two more fired, and he fell.

"The hillside was now alive with shouting and yelling savages. Our boat reached the middle of the stream and drifted down, the Indians all the while running along the shore and pouring in a continual fire. Two more of our crew were wounded. We had drifted down about half a mile, when we ran upon a sand bar within rifle range of the shore.

"The savages, supposing that they had their prey secure, gave utterance to the most appalling yells I ever heard. They came down to the water's edge, and, lying down on the sand, poured a continuous rain of bullets into us.

"We knew that unless we could get off the bar we should be compelled to surrender, for our ammunition would soon be exhausted, and then the Indians would swim to us, and come aboard our boat.

"Four of us volunteered to leap into the water and push the boat off the bar. We leaped in on the opposite side from the Indians, and keeping under as much as possible, we crawled around to the bow, placed our shoulders against the boat, and lifted and pushed until I thought I could see stars. At last the boat broke ground and drifted away into deep water, leaving us four behind. One of the men, named Joe Sapp, could not swim a stroke. The Indians' bullets were whizzing thick as bees about our heads, and we decided that we must somehow get to the boat.

"Bennet and Briggs, who were strong swimmers, told Sapp to place a hand on the back of each, and hold to them, and they would carry him to the boat. They did so. I followed after them, and we all climbed on board.

"The Indians followed us for seven miles down the

stream, keeping up a continuous fire. Though we had none killed, we had five men wounded, and were delayed two weeks at Franklin before we could proceed up the river."

The savages often captured and robbed the boats on their way down or on their return up the river. Many artifices were resorted to in order to draw the boats in to shore.

Once a St. Louis keel boat bound for New Orleans was drifting down the stream, when a man was seen on shore making frantic signals for it to land and take him on board. He wore a hat slouched over his eyes, and as he sat on the bank he kept dipping his hand into the water, apparently washing a wound on his face.

The keel boat began to put in to shore, when one of the crew said, —

"Maybe it is a trick to decoy us."

"How?"

"It may be an Indian in white men's clothes."

"I have a spyglass in my cabin. I will get it and see," said the captain.

When he had leveled his glass on the person on shore, he saw a dark hand in the water, and a moment later the head was raised so that he could see the face. Sure enough, it was an Indian in the clothes of a white man.

Then, turning his glass, the captain discovered heads and rifle barrels peeping out from behind the bushes and trees. He ordered the man at the helm to turn the prow toward the opposite shore, and the sweeps were manned. The boat glided over to the other side of the stream and escaped the trap set for it.

The danger, toil, and hardships of the western boatman were numerous, yet there was a peculiar fascination about the life which caused many to adopt it. These men played an important part in the settlement of Missouri. But the magic influence of steam has done away with the keel-boat system, and that brave, hardy race, once familiar in every river town, has passed away.

XIV.

THE BLOCKHOUSE AT THE BIG SPRING.

THERE is in St. Louis County a place known as the Big Spring. Soon after the territory was purchased by the United States, a few families from Virginia and Kentucky settled near it. Their numbers increased until quite a settlement grew up.

The Osages, Pottawatomies, and Iowa Indians frequently came down the river in canoes to annoy the settlers at this place. They would come in small thieving bands, and plunder indiscriminately. This annoyance, together with the alarm felt over the fate of Bouvet and the killing of others, caused the people at the Big Spring to build a blockhouse.

Blockhouses were not all alike. This one was made of logs, as usual, but the second story was laid cornerwise on the first, so that ports could be made to cover not only the sides, but the corners as well. The portholes were not over a foot square, and were provided with blocks of wood with which they could be plugged up after the riflemen had fired, in order to make the people secure while they were reloading.

Rumors of Indians in the vicinity very much alarmed the settlers at the Big Spring, and a request was sent to St. Louis for soldiers to guard the blockhouse.

Twenty privates under a lieutenant were accordingly detailed for this duty.

The presence of the garrison, instead of allaying the fears of the people, increased them. The soldiers seemed to be positive evidence of danger.

There was in the blockhouse a timid young lady named Fugate, who, unlike most frontier girls, was subject to fainting fits. She supposed that the soldiers would know all about the Indians, and that they were the proper persons to appeal to for information. Timidly approaching the sentry on duty, she asked,—

"Do you think we are in any danger, Mr. Soldier?"

The sentry, in a spirit of mischief, answered, "Shouldn't be surprised, madam, if we weren't all dead before morning."

With a shriek, Miss Fugate swooned, and was carried to her room. During the night she suffered from hysterics, and her friends feared she would die of fright. The anxiety and dread of the people in the fort were so great that they slept little.

Several days passed, and, as no Indians appeared, the soldiers returned to St. Louis, while the people went back to their homes and resumed the work on their farms.

One morning, two settlers named Clark and Beddington, while going to the river, were astonished to see half a dozen canoes filled with Indians paddling in to shore. They at once hurried back to the settlement and warned everybody that they saw.

"Go to the blockhouse, run to the blockhouse; the Indians are coming!" was the general cry. Two or

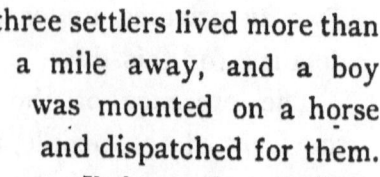

three settlers lived more than a mile away, and a boy was mounted on a horse and dispatched for them. Before the Indians reached the Big Spring settlement, the whites were all within the blockhouse, and had most of their live stock within an inclosure sufficiently near to protect them. There are conflicting reports as to the number of the attacking force. Some say there were but sixteen, others say there were thirty-two, while still others put the number at sixty.

The Indians had expected to surprise the white people, and had planned to leave the country as soon as they had taken a few scalps and had stolen such property as they could conveniently lay their hands on. It was a great disappointment to find the intended victims in their stronghold.

The blockhouse was in a grove of trees, and the savages, taking shelter behind these, opened fire. The shots were returned, and for a while the volleys made it seem as if a battle were raging.

Most of the women were as cool as the men, and stood by, molding bullets and loading guns. But

Miss Fugate was no pioneer. The crack of rifles shattered her nerves, and after swooning two or three times she became frantic with hysterics.

No one within the blockhouse was killed, and but two or three were wounded, and those not seriously. It is not known if any of the Indians were killed. None were found after the fight, but the savages had a way of carrying off their dead and wounded. In connection with this attack, there is a story told which illustrates the cunning of the Indians. A boy saw a savage creeping through the bushes and tall grass on the south side in order to get into a better position. He fired, and the Indian fell.

"I've killed one of them! I've killed one of them!" the lad shouted joyfully.

An old hunter named Crow, who thoroughly understood the tricks of the wily red man, said,—

"Don't be too sure, Jess. Watch him until I get my gun loaded."

"What are you going to do?" the boy asked, when he saw Mr. Crow aiming at the fallen brave. "Don't go to wasting lead on a dead Indian."

"Wait and see," was all the answer that the old hunter made.

The Indian lay in the grass so that only a part of one shoulder was visible. The white man aimed at that part and fired. The fallen brave leaped to his feet with a yell of pain, and, clapping his hand to his wounded shoulder, ran howling away.

"There goes your dead Indian," said Mr. Crow, with a laugh.

After that, whenever the boy was inclined to boast of his skill with a rifle, he was silenced by some one asking if he had not slain an Indian at the blockhouse.

Finding it impossible to capture the white men's stronghold by storm, and fearing reinforcements from St. Louis, the Indians, after killing some cows and hogs in the woods, hurried to their canoes and paddled up the river. The blockhouse was never again attacked.

XV.

THE LEWIS AND CLARK EXPEDITION.

JUST before the transfer of Louisiana to the United States, in 1803, President Jefferson was preparing to send out an exploring expedition into the territory which now comprises the northwestern part of the United States. Beyond Indian tradition, that region was then unknown.

The President's suggestions had been approved by Congress, and in January, 1803, he commissioned Captains Meriwether Lewis and William Clark to explore the Missouri River and its principal branches to their fountain heads. They were then to seek and trace to its termination in the Pacific, some stream which might give the most direct and practicable water communication across the continent, for purposes of navigation.

At that time railroads were unknown, and navigable streams were the only means by which commerce could be extensively carried on.

The expedition of Lewis and Clark was of the utmost importance to Missouri. It resulted in a definite knowledge of the great West, and in the subsequent pushing of settlements and trading posts farther into the interior.

Shortly after Lewis and Clark received their orders,

the news of the conclusion of the Louisiana purchase reached the United States. In May, 1804, these two officers came to St. Louis with thirty soldiers, a number of guides, and all the necessary supplies. Boats suitable for the long journey were constructed. They were of a peculiar make, long and narrow, strong and light, and capable of floating in shallow water. They were provided with sweeps, and with light masts which could be taken down when not needed. The best workmen obtainable were employed in their construction, and few boats have had greater care expended on them.

The work was pushed forward so rapidly that the expedition was ready before the end of the month. Then, on the day set for its departure, the whole town of St. Louis turned out to see the bold explorers start; for their journey was to take them thousands of miles through the wilderness.

It was one of the most hazardous undertakings of the time, and it required men of great courage and strength. The party was made up of picked men, inured to the privations and dangers of the West. Yet many thought, when the little party started, that it would never return. Not only were hostile Indians to be met, but there were a thousand other dangers to be confronted in the great wilderness.

As the boats glided under easy sail up the broad bosom of the Mississippi, a salute was fired from the fort, handkerchiefs were waved, and the people along the shore gave them many hearty cheers.

When they entered the mouth of the Missouri, navigation became more difficult. This river is narrower and more crooked than the Mississippi, and the current is much swifter. The explorers were compelled, for the most part, either to depend upon their sweeps, or else to cordelle their boats along the river banks, both of which ways were slow and toilsome.

The party reached St. Charles, and rested one day. This was the last landmark of civilization. Beyond, all was a dense and unexplored wilderness.

Slowly up the dark stream the boats glided, day after day. All signs of frontier settlements gave way to great forests, hills, and prairies. Sometimes there were towering bluffs on each side of the stream; sometimes level tracts of forests, and sometimes vast bottoms covered with tall wild grass. Occasionally, a deer forced its way through the mass of tall grass and tangled bushes and vines, and paused on the bank to gaze on the strange procession that was passing up the stream.

On June 7, 1804, the explorers reached the mouth of Bonne Femme Creek (Good Woman Creek) in Howard County, a few miles below where the city of Boonville now stands. Being considerably wearied with their journey, they did not move their camp all next day, but explored the river bottom as far back as the mouth of the Moniteau, a stream that empties into the Missouri at the southeastern corner of Howard County.

At this place there was a lofty bluff and a projecting point of rocks. These were covered with those strange and mysterious hieroglyphic Indian paintings which have baffled all interpretation.

While Clark was climbing up a rocky ledge in order

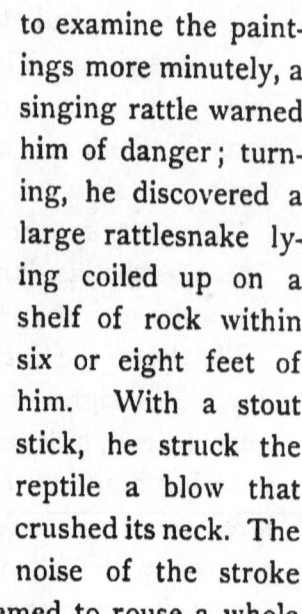

to examine the paintings more minutely, a singing rattle warned him of danger; turning, he discovered a large rattlesnake lying coiled up on a shelf of rock within six or eight feet of him. With a stout stick, he struck the reptile a blow that crushed its neck. The noise of the stroke seemed to rouse a whole colony of rattlesnakes. From crevices in the rock, from behind stones, and among bushes there started up such an army of them that Clark and those with him gave up all thought of further investigation, and, retreating hurriedly down the bluff, returned to their camp.

Next day they resumed their toilsome journey up the Missouri. They traveled through the heart of the State, and along the northwestern border. Sixteen hundred miles from St. Louis, they went into winter quarters among the Mandan Indians. In April of the next year, they passed the mouth of the Yellowstone River. Crossing the Rocky Mountains, they entered the head waters of the Columbia, and floated down that stream to its mouth in the Pacific. They spent the winter on the south bank of the Columbia, and in the spring set out on their homeward journey.

In September, 1806, Lewis and Clark arrived with their party in St. Louis, after an absence of over two years, during which they had traveled more than eight thousand miles. On their return, two of the guides, named Colter and Potts, obtained permission to remain on the Missouri and trap for beaver. Knowing the hostility of the Indians, they used to put out their traps at night, and take them up in the morning, remaining concealed during the day.

Early one morning, they were ascending a creek to examine their traps, when they heard a noise like the tramping of wild animals.

"That noise was made by Indians, and we had better retreat," said Colter.

"Oh, it was a herd of buffalo," declared Potts. "Come, don't be a coward."

They proceeded up the creek, but had not gone two hundred yards when four or five hundred Indians appeared on the banks, and began to beckon them to come on shore.

As retreat was impossible, Colter turned the head of the canoe in to shore. The moment the craft touched the bank, an Indian seized the gun belonging to Potts. Colter, who was a very strong man, took it away from him and gave it back to Potts, who had remained in the canoe. On receiving the gun, Potts pushed off into the stream, but he had scarcely left the shore when an arrow struck him.

"Colter, I am wounded," he cried.

"Don't try to escape, but come back to shore," said his comrade.

Instead of taking this advice, Potts leveled his gun at the Indian who had wounded him, and shot the savage dead. In a moment, he was pierced by a dozen arrows, and expired. The Indians then seized Colter, stripped him entirely naked, and began to consult on the manner in which they should put him to death. Some favored tying him up as a target, and shooting him to death with their arrows.

The chief finally came to Colter, and, placing his hand on the captive's shoulder, asked him if he could run fast. The white man, who understood some of the Indian language, answered that he was a very poor runner. The truth was, he was considered remarkably swift by the hunters who knew him.

The chief commanded his warriors to remain where they were, and led Colter out on the prairie three or four hundred yards. Then he released the captive, bidding him save himself if he could. At that instant the war whoop sounded behind him, and, impelled by the hope of saving his life, he ran with a speed that surprised himself. Before him lay a prairie about six miles across, and beyond this was a heavy forest which bordered the banks of a stream. Colter felt that if he could reach the forest he would be safe.

When about halfway across the prairie, he ventured to glance back over his shoulder, and saw that the Indians were much scattered. He had gained on the most of them, but one who carried a spear was not more than a hundred yards behind him. With confidence in the possibility of escape, he increased his speed to the utmost. So great were his exertions, that the blood gushed from his nostril and soon almost covered the front of his body.

When within a mile of the river, Colter heard the sound of footsteps behind him. Glancing back, he saw the savage not twenty yards away. He stopped suddenly, turned around, and spread out his arms. The Indian, surprised at the action of Colter, and at the bloody appearance of his body, tried to stop and throw his spear. But he stumbled and fell, his spear sticking into the ground and breaking off in his hand.

Colter seized the pointed part of the weapon, pinned the savage to the earth, and then continued his flight. He reached the creek, plunged in, and concealed himself under a pile of driftwood, with his body submerged in the water. The Indians were soon all over the drift, searching for him, but he remained in his hiding place all day. At night, naked and unarmed as he was, he came out and started off to seek white people. For seven days he traveled, subsisting on wild berries and roots which he dug out of the earth with his hands.

White people were reached at last, and he was saved.

XVI.

PIKE IN NORTHEAST MISSOURI.

ABOUT the time that President Jefferson appointed Lewis and Clark to explore the Missouri, Lieutenant Zebulon Pike, for whom Pikes Peak is named, was appointed to explore the upper Mississippi.

In the afternoon of Friday, August 9, 1805, Lieutenant Pike left St. Louis in a keel boat seventy feet long, with provisions for four months. He was accompanied by a crew, one sergeant, seventeen privates, and one interpreter. This was the first expedition up the Mississippi that was sent out by the United States government.

In 1810, Lieutenant Pike published a little book describing his journey into northeast Missouri. Although only twenty-five years of age, he had the wisdom of a much older man. He kept a diary in which was a careful record of every incident of the journey, even to catching a few fish or losing a dog.

On August 15, 1805, he passed the mouth of Salt River, where he says he "left another dog." The Indian name of Salt River was Auhahah or Oahahah. Pike gives us in his diary a brief description of this and the neighboring rivers as they then appeared.

"Salt River bears from the Mississippi north 75°

west, and is about one hundred or one hundred and twenty yards wide at its entrance. When I passed, it appeared to be perfectly mild, with scarcely any current. About one day's sail up the river, there are salt springs, which have been worked for four years; but I am not informed as to their qualities or productions. In this distance, the navigation of the Mississippi is very much obstructed by bars and islands; indeed, to such a degree as to render it difficult to find (in many places) a proper channel. The shores are generally a sandy soil, timbered with sugar maple, ash, pecan, locust, and black walnut.

"The east side has generally the preference as to situations for building. From this to the river Jauflione (which is our boundary between the Sac Nation and the United States on the west side of the Mississippi) we have the hills on the west shore, and the lowlands on the east, the latter of which are timbered with hickory, oak, ash, maple, pecan, etc.; the former the same with an increase of oak. The east is a rich sandy soil, and has many eligible situations for cultivation.

"About seven miles below the Jauflione a Frenchman is settled on the west shore. He is married to a woman of the Sac Nation, and lives by a little cultivation and the Indian trade.

"The river before mentioned is about thirty yards wide at its mouth, and bears from the Mississippi about southwest. In this part the river navigation is good. From this to the Wyaconda River the navigation is easy, with very few impediments, and the soil on both sides is pretty good. This river pays its tribute to the

Mississippi by a mouth one hundred yards wide, and bears from the latter nearly due west. Just below its entrance is a small stream fifteen yards wide which discharges itself into the Mississippi."

The Frenchman with the Indian wife, whom Pike mentioned, was living in Marion County, Missouri, and was no doubt the first white settler in that part of the State. Pike wrote of him,—

"His cattle were in fine order, but his corn was in a bad state of cultivation. About one mile above his house, on the west shore, is a very handsome hill, which he (the Frenchman) informed me is level on the top, with a gradual descent on either side, and a fountain of fine water. This man likewise told me that two men had been killed on the Big Bay or Three Brothers, and he desired to be informed what measures had been taken in consequence thereof. We encamped four miles above his house."

Next day the party made thirty-nine miles without any incident worthy of special mention, except passing three *bateaux*, probably belonging to trappers and traders. The day following they were fired on by some Indians on the Illinois shore, and were driven over to the Missouri side. On the 19th an accident happened to their boat which delayed them so that they made but fourteen miles that day. Next day they reached the Des Moines rapids and were beyond Missouri.

The stream called by Pike the Jauflione was afterwards known as the Jefferion, and is now called the Fabius. No stream in Missouri has been known by more names. Some old writers call it the Geoffrion, and one authority is of the opinion that its original name was Javelot. The last is a French word signifying a spear, and doubtless the Indian name was of the same meaning.

The name Fabius is said to be derived from a Spanish word meaning a pea or bean. When the stream was discovered, a great quantity of wild peas grew along its banks.

In time the south fork of the stream was called the Little Fabba, and many old settlers in Missouri still speak of the two streams as the Fabbas.

Their wooded shores became historic during the Civil War. They afforded hiding places for the partisan soldiery of the Confederate army, and many a hot skirmish was fought along their banks.

XVII.

CAPTAIN COLE.—A PLUCKY FRENCH-WOMAN.

EARLY in the history of St. Charles County, preparations were made for defense against the Indians. Companies of rangers were organized, and a number of forts were erected.

Each of the forts was built in the form of a parallelogram, with blockhouses at the four corners, and with the sides consisting of log cabins and thick palisades. They were strong enough to resist muskets and rifles, but would have been small protection against artillery. Besides affording protection from the Indians, each fort became the nucleus of a little settlement, which ultimately grew into a village or thriving district.

In 1806 or 1807, a few American families settled on Loutre Island. This island is in the Missouri River, just at the mouth of Loutre Creek, and the settlement on it was among the most exposed of any on the Missouri border at that time.

In the year 1807 a band of ten Indians, Sacs and Pottawatomies, came from Iowa and the northern part of Missouri, stole seven horses belonging to the inhabitants of Loutre Island, and then fled northward with them. Five settlers started in pursuit. They were

William Temple Cole, Stephen Cole, James Patton, John Gooch, and James Murdock.

On the evening of the second day out, the party came in sight of the Indians on the Salt River Prairie, in what is now the southern part of Ralls County. The white men moved forward a mile or so, and then, as darkness was coming on, they went into camp in a dense wood on the bank of Spencer Creek, intending to open friendly negotiations with the Indians on the following morning.

Two of the men remained on guard while the others slept. They little dreamed that the sharp eyes of the Indians were upon their camp. The night was dark, and while they slept the savages surrounded them. Suddenly, the cracks of rifles and the most appalling yells rose on the air. W. T. Cole and Gooch were instantly killed. Patton was wounded, but started up on his knees, when a shot laid him dead on his blanket.

Stephen Cole and Murdock seized their rifles and fired into the darkness. Murdock leaped through the thicket and dropped down under the bank of the creek, then crawled on hands and knees a long distance up the stream, and escaped. After wandering several days in the forest and prairie, he at last reached Loutre Island.

Stephen Cole was left alone to battle with the savages. He was a large, powerful, and very brave man. Two of the Indians threw themselves upon him, and engaged him in a hand-to-hand fight. Knocking down the Indian in front, Cole turned upon one that had wounded him in the back. Seizing his wrist, the white man wrung the knife from the Indian's hand, and drove it into his heart up to the hilt.

The dying yell of the savage called the remaining eight Indians to the spot. In the darkness it was difficult to tell friend from foe. The white man struck right and left, and inflicted some ugly wounds on his enemies. He succeeded in cutting his way through, then leaped over the bank of the creek, and, aided by the darkness, made his escape. Mr. Cole's wound was painful, but not dangerous. He traveled day and night through the woods, until finally Loutre Island was reached.

The wounded man at once organized a company to go with him to the place where his companions had been slain. His friends tried to dissuade him from returning, but in vain. As soon as his wound was dressed, he placed himself at the head of a party of armed settlers, and set out for the scene of the late conflict. The dead were found and buried, but the Indians had fled from that part of the country.

In after years, no name was more familiar on the Missouri frontier than that of Captain Stephen Cole. It was he who, in 1812, built Cole's Fort, and it was for him that Cole County was named. He was killed by the Indians in 1824 while returning from Santa Fé, with which town the people in Missouri had opened a brisk trade.

* * * * * * *

From its exposed position, vast territory, and sparse population, north Missouri suffered more from Indian depredations, in the early history of the Territory, than any other part of the country. With few exceptions, the Indians on the Missouri River were peaceable, even during the War of 1812. The northern Indians, however, including the Sacs, Pottawatomies, and Iowas, made frequent incursions into the inhabited portions of the Territory. They would murder and plunder, and then, as soon as they were pursued by rangers, they would flee to the north.

One of the most noted conflicts of the early Indian wars was at Cote Sans Dessein, a French settlement in what is now Callaway County, two miles below the mouth of the Osage River. The blockhouse was built on a limestone hill, six hundred yards long, in a piece of bottom land. The hill was a vast and isolated mound, and hence its name, which means a "Hill without Design," or an unaccountable hill.

Cote Sans Dessein was once a village of considerable importance. Early in the War of 1812, it was attacked by a large body of Indians. At the time of the attack the blockhouse was occupied only by a Frenchman named Baptiste Louis Roi, with two other men and two women; but these five persons successfully resisted the determined siege until the rangers from St. Louis came to their relief.

The Frenchmen were cool, and, being experienced marksmen, brought down a man at almost every shot. The blockhouse was easily defended, because of its position on the hill, and because there was little underbrush and few trees near by to protect the attacking party. While the men fired through the portholes at the savages, the women molded bullets and loaded guns. Roi was the hero of the fight, but his wife was no less heroic than himself.

The Indians, knowing that there were not many in the defending party, tried to storm the fort. Roi discovered their design, and ordered all to withhold their fire until the enemy were within a few yards. Then he gave the order, and the guns flashed with such deadly effect that the savages turned about and fled down the hill.

They next tried to burn the blockhouse. Fastening combustibles on their arrows, they shot them into the roof, which in a few moments was on fire.

"I'll put it out," cried the brave Madame Roi. "Shoot the savages, and mind not the blazing roof." Seizing a bucket of water, she climbed up by means of an inside ladder, and extinguished the flames. The conflict still raged. Again and again was the roof set in flames by burning arrows, and as often did the heroic Frenchwoman extinguish them.

But at last the supply of water was exhausted, and another flaming arrow had stuck in the roof. The fort was on fire, and the band of rangers who were expected from St. Louis had not yet come. Even Roi began to despair.

One of the men, peering out from a porthole at this moment, descried the St. Louis rangers coming, but they were still some distance away. The fort would be in ashes before they could reach it. If those flames could be once more extinguished, the defenders would be saved. Madame Roi was equal to the emergency.

She ran to her cupboard, and, taking from it a pan of milk, once more flew up the ladder and put out the fire.

The yells of the disappointed savages had scarcely ceased to reverberate among the hills and forests, when the relief party burst upon them like a tornado. The Indians fled, and Cote Sans Dessein was saved by a plucky Frenchwoman.

XVIII.

MISSOURI RANGERS.

THE early struggles with the Indians in Missouri called into existence a class of military men known as rangers. They were hardy and fearless, always ready for some daring enterprise, and willing to undergo any amount of toil and hardship to defend the frontier. Their discipline and manner of service differed from those of the regular army, and most of them served without pay. Though they were divided into companies and regiments, no record has been preserved of their organization; if any was made, it was destroyed when the State capitol burned, about twenty-five years later.

Each ranger furnished his own horse, arms, and ammunition. The rations were sometimes provided at the expense of the general government, but often the men had to depend on the wild game of the forest for their food. As there is no record of the early Missouri rangers, we are dependent upon tradition for their history.

In 1870, there was still living in Ralls County an old ranger, eighty-four years of age. His name was Richard Chitwood, and to him and a few others of his class the present generation is indebted for much information of those early soldiers.

According to Mr. Chitwood, the first regiment of rangers was organized and commanded by Colonel David Musick, of St. Louis, who was one of the first representatives from that county in the Territorial Legislature. Among his most daring men was his nephew, Asa, of whom many stories are told. The young man was foolhardy in danger, yet came through a score of pitched battles and hard-fought skirmishes unharmed.

One day, while a small party of rangers was scouting in the woods near the Osage, some Indians were seen to enter a group of trees. The rangers hesitated to attack them, but Asa sprang from his horse and crawled almost to the thicket, when the Indians suddenly leaped out of it, and ran toward the river. Asa fired his rifle at them; then, throwing it on the ground, he pursued the savages to the banks of the Osage, with no weapon but his knife. He would even have followed them across the river if he had not been prevented by his companions.

On another occasion, the rangers were engaged in building a line of forts on the Missouri River in the St. Charles district, and were using a yoke of oxen to draw the logs from the forest. At night the oxen were unyoked and allowed to graze within the circle of camp guards. One night while Asa was on guard, the oxen escaped from the camp, and strayed into the woods. Colonel Musick, enraged at his nephew's carelessness, sent him into the woods to hunt for them. Asa came back after a few hours, and reported that he had been unable to find them.

"Go back!" cried the angry colonel, "and don't you dare to return until you have found that yoke of oxen."

Asa left the camp and went to Kentucky, where he remained five years. At the end of that time, he returned to St. Louis. The war was over, and the rangers had been discharged for some time. On inquiry, Asa learned that the colonel lived in the town, so he went to his house and knocked at the door. The colonel answered the summons, and was astonished at being confronted by the deserter of five years before. Asa gave him a serious look, and said, —

"I have come to tell you, Uncle Dave, that I haven't found the oxen."

* * * * * * * *

Another daring ranger of the time was Jerry Ball, who served in the same regiment as Asa did. He was one of the best marksmen on the frontier. His rifle, a long-barreled gun, was made for hunting bear, and it was said that he could send a bullet twice as far as any one else in the regiment.

Once while he was scouting with two or three others on the Missouri, they discovered some Indians across the river. The Indians, supposing themselves at a safe distance, began to make defiant gestures at the rangers. When Jerry Ball dismounted and took aim at them, they shouted in derision. He fired, and fatally wounded one of them, whereupon the others fled. For this feat Jerry was called by the Indians "Long Shot."

Though most of the rangers were men of reckless daring, there was occasionally one of quite the opposite character. We are told of a certain Harmon who was of this sort, and who, like most cowards, was a great boaster. When the rangers first started on their campaign, he insisted on riding in front.

Most of the rangers thought Harmon was very brave; but there was one old man who declared that he was a most consummate coward, and that he would show himself to be such when they came under fire. Harmon boasted so much of what he would do when they found the Indians, that some of his companions became tired of it, and determined to put his courage to a test.

All the company were taken into the secret except two or three of Harmon's most intimate friends. One evening after they had gone into camp, a dozen young men stole away unseen into the forest. Shortly after dark, rapid firing and deafening yells were heard on the right, and the sentries, running into the circle of light made by the camp fire, shouted, —

"Indians! Indians!"

Harmon ran. He did not stop to mount his horse, which had been picketed out to graze; he did not stop to put on his cap, which had fallen to the ground. A camp dog that stood in his way was kicked aside; and then the fleeing Harmon was seen to leap over logs, dodge under bushes, and plunge into a muddy swamp, sending the frightened frogs in every direction. According to one of the rangers who sometimes wrote doggerel verse, —

He kicked the dogs,
And leaped the logs,
And scared the frogs,
And plunged into the water.

Nor did Harmon stop there. He ran until he reached the nearest fort, about forty miles distant. On being asked where the others were, he answered, —

"All killed. The Indians have killed and scalped every one of them. I am all that is left to tell the tale."

The people in the fort were for several days in a state of alarm and anxiety; but this was changed to laughter when the company returned from a bloodless campaign, and related the joke that had been played on Harmon. The boaster was effectually cured of his bad habit, but never again went with the rangers.

Quite in contrast with Harmon was a ranger known as Little Abe. Though twenty-four years of age, he was so small that he was often mistaken for a boy. He kept his face shaved perfectly smooth, which added to his youthful appearance. Little Abe was among the most daring of the rangers, and was a fine marksman. He could bark a squirrel nine shots out of ten, a feat which was regarded as the most difficult of all to perform. To "bark a squirrel," the rifle must be aimed so that the ball will strike and shiver the bark of the limb on which the animal is crouching. The squirrel is thrown into the air as if by an explosion, and is killed by the concussion.

Another favorite feat of Little Abe's was snuffing a candle. This shot was always made after night. A lighted candle was placed on a stump fifty yards from the marksman. He would then take aim offhand, and shoot the top of the wick off; that is, actually snuff the candle without extinguishing the flame.

The rangers once started out to pursue a band of Indians that had come down from the northern part of the Territory. These savages had stolen a few horses, and then, according to their usual custom, had fled back toward their homes. The rangers had gone two days' forced march, when they ascertained that a party of Indians had slipped back past them. When last seen, this party was going in the direction of John Patton's house, which was two or three miles from the fort. Patton, who was with the company, became very much alarmed for his wife and children, whom he had left at home. When the rangers began the pursuit, no one thought of any savages getting in their rear and attacking the settlement which they had left. Now, however, they turned about, and hurried back as rapidly as their almost exhausted horses could go.

Ten miles from Patton's cabin, every horse except Little Abe's had given out. He pressed on alone, some of the others following on foot. A little before sunset, the ranger came in sight of the cabin, and saw fifteen or twenty Indians not over a fourth of a mile from it. Little Abe urged his tired horse to the top of its speed. When he reached the gate, he sprang from the saddle, leaped into the door, and quickly told Mrs. Patton why he had come.

Not dreaming of danger, Mrs. Patton had remained at home during her husband's absence. She was a brave woman. She first hastened to take her children to the attic, and then returned to assist in the defense. When Little Abe opened fire on the savages, Mrs. Patton took down a rifle that hung on the wall, gave it to him, and then reloaded the one he had emptied.

The cabin was so near to the fort that the firing was heard there, and a rescuing party was sent to drive the savages away. The remarkable skill and courage of Little Abe enabled him to keep the Indians at bay until help arrived. Three Indians were found dead on the ground.

XIX.

THE CAPTIVE.

THERE is no more beautiful and thrilling tale of early pioneer days, than the story of Helen Patterson. She was born in Kentucky; but while she was still a child her parents removed to St. Louis County, Missouri, and lived for a time in a settlement called Cold Water, which is in St. Ferdinand township. About the year 1808 or 1809, her father took his family to the St. Charles district, and settled only a few miles from the home of the veteran backwoodsman, Daniel Boone.

At the time of this last removal, Helen was about eighteen years of age. She was a very religious girl, and had been taught to believe that whatever she prayed for would be granted.

Shortly after the family had settled in their new home, bands of prowling savages began to roam about the neighborhood. The Indians would plunder the cabins of the settlers during their absence, and drive away their cattle, horses, and hogs.

One day, business called all the Patterson family to the village, except Helen. She was busily engaged in spinning, when the house was surrounded by nine Indians. Resistance was useless. She did not attempt to escape or even cry out for help; for one of the savages who spoke English gave her to understand that she would be killed if she did so.

She was told that she must follow the Indians. They took such things as they could conveniently carry, and with their captive set off on foot through the forest, in a northwestern direction. The shrewd girl had brought a ball of yarn with her, and from this she occasionally broke off a bit and dropped it at the side of the path, as a guide to her father and friends, who she knew would soon be in pursuit.

This came very near being fatal to Helen, for one of the Indians observed what she was doing, and raised his hatchet to brain her. The others interceded, but the ball of yarn was taken from her, and she was closely watched lest she might resort to some other device for marking a trail.

It was early in the morning when Helen was captured. Her parents were expected to return to the cabin by noon, and she reasoned that they would be in pursuit before the Indians had gone very far. As the savages were on foot, and her father would no doubt follow them on horseback, he might overtake them before dark. The uneasiness expressed by her captors during the afternoon encouraged her in the belief that her friends were in pursuit.

A little before sunset, two of the Indians went back to reconnoiter, and the other seven, with the captive, continued on in the forest. Shortly after sunset, the two Indians who had fallen behind joined the others, and all held a short consultation, which the white girl could not understand.

The conference lasted but a few moments, and then the savages hastened forward with Helen to a creek, where the banks were sloping, and the water shallow enough for them to wade the stream. By the time they had crossed, it was quite dark. The night was cloudy, and distant thunder could occasionally be heard.

The Indians hurried their captive to a place half a mile from the ford, and there tied her with strips of deerskin to one of the low branches of an elm. Her hands were extended above her head, and her wrists were crossed and tied so tightly that she found it impossible to release them. When they had secured her to their own satisfaction, the Indians left her, assuring her that they were going back to the ford to shoot her father and his companions as they crossed it.

Helen was almost frantic with fear and grief. Added to the uncertainty of her own fate was the knowledge that her father and friends were marching right into an Indian ambuscade.

In the midst of her trouble, she did not forget her pious teaching. She prayed God to send down his angels and release her. But no angel came. In her distress, the rumbling thunders in the distance were unheard, and she hardly noticed the shower until she was drenched to the skin.

The rain thoroughly wet the strips of deerskin with which she was tied, and as they stretched she almost unconsciously slipped her hands from them. Her prayer had been answered by the rain. She hastily untied her feet, and sped away toward the creek. Guided by the lightning's friendly glare, she crossed the stream half a mile above the ford, and hastened to meet her father and friends.

At every flash of lightning she strained her eyes, hoping to catch sight of them. At last, moving forms were seen in the distance, but they were too far away for her to determine whether they were white men or Indians. Crouching down at the root of a tree by the path, she waited until they were within a few rods of her, and then cried in a low voice, —

"Father! Father!"

"That is Helen," said Mr. Patterson.

She bounded to her feet, and in a moment was at his side, telling him how she had escaped. The rescuing party was composed of her father and two brothers, a neighbor named Shultz, and Nathan and Daniel M. Boone, sons of the great pioneer, Daniel Boone.

She told them where the Indians were lying in ambush, and the frontiersmen decided to surprise them. They crossed the creek on a log, and stole down to the ford, but the Indians were gone. No doubt the savages had discovered the escape of the prisoner, and, knowing that their plan to surprise the white men had failed, became frightened and fled.

Helen Patterson always believed it was her prayers that saved her father, her brothers, and herself in that trying hour.

XX.

BOONE'S SALT WORKS.

TRANSPORTING goods to Missouri in the early days was very expensive, and the inhabitants soon learned to manufacture many of the things they needed. Among the earliest of their products was salt.

Hunters, trappers, and traders who went into the wilderness discovered springs which were so briny that they could not drink the water. Deer, elk, and buffalo frequented these springs to lick the salt deposited around them. For that reason, the banks were called "salt licks"; and hunters used to watch these places for the game which came to them.

When the first salt was made in Missouri, is not definitely known. Several places and several persons claim the honor. The early method of making salt was simple enough. Kettles were filled with brine, which was boiled until it had all evaporated, leaving only the salt. Early in the history of Missouri, even before the Spanish had transferred the country to the United States, salt was thus made by settlers. It was not until later years, however, that this became a lucrative business.

In February, 1804, Ira P. Nash and two companions went up the Missouri River and located the first claim on public lands in what is now Howard County. They remained there almost a month, and while hunting discovered some springs that were rich with salt.

The sons of Daniel Boone, Nathan and Daniel M. Boone, were noted for their courage and enterprise. They heard of the wonderful salt springs in the "upper country," or country up the Missouri River, and in 1806 they set out to examine them. Arriving in what is now Howard County, they selected a location for salt works.

During the summer of 1807, the Boone brothers, with three men named Goforth, Baldridge, and Manly, took a large number of kettles, and went up the Missouri River in boats to manufacture salt at the place which they had located. Being compelled to row against the current, their journey was slow and laborious. It was the more so on account of the great caution they were obliged to use in ascending the river, for the dark, muddy stream was filled with hidden snags, rocks, and sand bars.

Arrived at the salt springs, they built furnaces, placed their kettles over them, and began making salt. The place was soon known as Boones Lick, and all the country above Cedar Creek was called the Boones Lick country. It is this Cedar Creek which now forms the boundary line between Callaway and Boone counties; at that time it was regarded as the western boundary of the district of St. Charles.

Sometime about 1809, five men left St. Charles with their kettles in a boat, drifted down the Missouri to its mouth, and then ascended the Mississippi as far as the mouth of Salt River. They went up this stream until they came to a salt spring in what is now Ralls County. Here, at what was known as Freemores Lick, they built a furnace, dug a well, and began making salt.

During the summer they were attacked by Indians, and compelled to leave their works. They threw their kettles into the well, and started for St. Charles. All but one were killed on the way. The man who escaped journeyed all the way to St. Charles through the forest and across the prairie without eating or sleeping until he reached his home.

Boone's sons, however, were unmolested, and in the fall they returned to St. Charles with canoes filled with salt. This led others to brave the dangers of the forest in order to share in the new industry. The Boones, however, were the chief salt makers of the time. They were bold, and the Indians feared them more than they did any one else. The name their father had gained was enough to inspire the savages with dread of the sons.

The explorations in the salt districts were fruitful of other results. The salt makers and explorers brought back intelligence of a beautiful country. They told of noble streams, grand forests, rolling prairies, and rich soils, and kindled in the hearts of the people a desire to live in that far-away land. Bold pioneers pushed out into the wilderness, and in a short time settlements began to spring up all over the Boones Lick country.

It was a large district, requiring three or four days to cross it on horseback, then the chief mode of travel. After the first settlement was made in Howard County, other settlers soon moved into the Boones Lick country, and by the year 1812 there were many small settlements here, besides a number of pioneers living at considerable distances from any of them.

The highway which led to what afterwards became the town of Old Franklin was known as the Boones Lick road. It became the main thoroughfare, and was made suitable for wagons.

At one place on this road there lived a pioneer whose nearest neighbor was ten miles distant. His cabin fronted the road, and his wife, lonely in her prairie home, was in the habit of hailing every passer-by, and asking, "What's the news?"

She soon became famous all over the Boones Lick country as the great interrogator. When the War of 1812 broke out, and the Missourians began to fear an attack from the British and Indians, her desire to learn the news increased.

The most terrifying stories were told at that time, and were believed by some. The whole country, for instance, would quickly become alarmed at the report that Brock and Tecumseh were on their march to the Missouri River, with a large army of British and Indians.

After a time, most of the frontiersmen learned to

discredit these reports; but the old lady in the lonely cabin still believed everything she heard. A man who had been stopped repeatedly on his way to and from the Boones Lick salt works, and asked if there was any news, determined to test this woman's credulity to the utmost.

The next time he rode past her house, she ran to the gate, as usual, and called, —

"Stop, Mr. Sinks, what's the news of the Indians?"

Mr: Sinks assumed a very serious look and answered, —

"Bad, madam, very bad. I am going to get my family out of the country just as soon as possible."

"Why, what's the trouble?"

"Tecumseh and his Indians have put handspikes under Lake Michigan, and are going to upset it and drown us all."

Wringing her hands, and shrieking in an agony of dread, the woman ran to the field where her husband was at work, and urged him to pack up and leave the country before they were drowned. When he learned what was the cause of her alarm, he declared that he didn't believe the Indians could upset the lake if they tried, and that, as he was a good swimmer, he was going to run the chances of getting out, if they did.

Portions of the Boones Lick country were for a long time subject to the raids of the Indians. During the winter, the savages remained in their villages and wigwams, living on the product of the summer's hunt and the labor of the women. But as soon as it was warm enough for them to leave their homes, they began to rob and murder the settlers on the frontier. In May, 1818, a band of them from the northern part of the State slipped down to the Boones Lick country, and approached the house of a pioneer named Ramsey.

Mrs. Ramsey was milking her cows, and was not aware of the presence of Indians until they fired at her. She dropped her milking pail and ran toward the house. They fired at her again, and one bullet wounded her; but she managed to reach the cabin before she fell.

Three of the children, who were in the front yard, were tomahawked and scalped. Mr. Ramsey was seriously wounded, but he managed to seize his rifle and keep the savages from the house.

Two of the boys escaped and gave the alarm; and the frontiersmen were not slow in rallying to the rescue. Among those who came to the scene was the old pioneer, Daniel Boone. He washed and dressed the wounds of Mrs. Ramsey, and made the last hours of the dying woman as comfortable as possible. When volunteers set out after the Indians, his eyes flashed with the same fire that had inspired him in his younger days, and he said, —

"I should like to go with you, boys, but I am no account any more."

The Indians were overtaken, four of them killed, and several wounded. Mrs. Ramsey died from her injuries, and was buried by the side of her children who had been killed on the day that she received her wounds.

XXI.[1]

COOPER AND CALLAWAY.

AS said before, the Boones Lick country was settled soon after its exploration. The first to make his home there was Colonel Benjamin Cooper.

With his wife and five sons, this pioneer came from Madison County, Kentucky, and in 1808 built a cabin near Boones Lick. Their immigration, like that of many other families, was a result of the search for salt, which was being industriously carried on. They had heard the stories about fertile soil, great forests, and abundant game, and were induced by them to brave all dangers and become the first settlers of what is now Howard County.

Colonel Cooper's location was so far beyond any other settlement, that he and his family were in great danger from the Indians. For this reason the governor of the Territory ordered him to live somewhere below the Gasconade River until he could be assured of some protection in his new home. The colonel obeyed the order, and moved to Loutre Island, where he remained for more than a year. In February, 1810, a number of other emigrants from Madison County, Kentucky, came

[1] The material for this chapter is partly from Col. W. F. Switzler's "History of Missouri."

to this same place, looking for homes in the new Territory. Cooper at once began to praise the Boones Lick country, and before the month was out he had induced a band of the sturdy pioneers to accompany him and his family to this much-desired locality. They traveled through a trackless forest, on the north side of the Missouri River, and safely reached their destination in March. The wives of the new immigrants did not arrive until August.

It did not take long for the settlers to build their cabin homes and clear enough land for cultivation; but the hostile Indians were a constant menace to the prosperity of the settlement. The Pottawatomies, who were the great horse thieves of the frontier, made frequent raids upon the Boones Lick country. In addition to this, the more warlike Iowas, Foxes, and Kickapoos threatened the lives of the settlers. For several years the little band of whites were obliged to rely wholly on themselves for protection; and in 1812 they built five forts. These were Cooper's Fort, Kinkaid's Fort, Fort Hempstead, Fort Head, and Cole's Fort. The four first named were all within what is now Howard County; but Cole's Fort was on the south side of the river, not far from where Boonville now stands. It was built and commanded by Stephen Cole, who, with Hannah Cole and their families, was the first to settle in Cooper County.

The settlers' cornfields were cultivated in common, and were near these strongholds. Sentinels were kept around the fields while the men were at work in them. At the first sign of danger, horns were blown, and all the people ran to the forts, where they were safe from

Indian attacks. In spite of all caution and bravery, however, a dozen or more settlers, at different times, were slain by the savages.

One dark, stormy night, Captain Sarshell Cooper was sitting in his own room in Cooper's Fort. His youngest child was on his knee, and his other children were playing on the floor about him. An Indian, knowing him to be a leading spirit among the whites, determined to kill him. Through driving rain and howling wind, the savage crept to the north of Captain Cooper's cabin, which formed one side of the fort. Carefully making a hole between two of the logs, just large enough to admit the muzzle of his gun, he took aim at Captain Cooper and fired. The brave frontiersman fell dead upon the floor, and his assassin fled to the forest and escaped. Thus perished the man for whom Cooper County was named.

* * * * * * * *

In the winter of 1812, Thomas Massey left Fort Clemison, on Loutre Island, where he had settled in 1809, and moved with his family to what was called Loutre Lick, where he had leased some land of Colonel Nathan Boone. Mr. Massey built a cabin on the north side of a little stream known as Sallies Branch, and cleared a small field on the south side. This field is now the site of the village of Mineola. One morning the father went up Loutre Creek to examine some Indian "signs" (or footprints) which he had discovered the previous day. Before going, he set his son Harris to plowing in the field.

"Carry your rifle on your back, while at work," said Mr. Massey, "and if you see an Indian, shoot him and run to the house." The boy slung his gun across his shoulder by a strap, and began plowing. But the gun was heavy, and after a while he set it against a tree.

About ten in the morning, a band of Sac Indians slyly came down Sallies Branch, and, crawling under the bank, approached within a hundred yards of the boy at work in the field. They shot him, and then ran up and scalped him.

From the cabin door, the mother and sister witnessed this terrible deed. Ann Massey, the oldest daughter, seized the dinner horn and blew such a blast that the Indians, fearing that the signal was for a band of white men, became alarmed and fled. Mr. Massey heard the firing and the dinner horn, and hastened home. The Indians had left the horses, and upon these he mounted his family, and set out at once for Fort Clemison, eighteen miles away. From that post, a party went to Mr. Massey's house and buried the dead boy.

On March 6, 1815, a band of seventy-five or eighty Sac and Fox Indians came down from the northern part of the Territory, and stole a dozen or more horses that were grazing on the mainland near Loutre Island. They hurried away, and succeeded in escaping with their stolen property up Loutre Creek. Captain James Callaway, with fifteen rangers, set out at once after the thieves. On the second day, they came upon a fresh trail left by the Indians. Rapidly following it, about two o'clock in the afternoon they came upon the camp, where they found the stolen horses, guarded by a few squaws. All the men were absent, and at sight of the rangers the Indian women fled. Captain Callaway did not pursue them, but collected the horses and started with them toward Loutre Island.

Lieutenant Jonathan Riggs, of the rangers, was an old Indian fighter, and a man of caution and judgment. His suspicions were aroused by the disappearance of the savages. He thought that they had dispersed in order to mislead the white men, and that they would make a circuit in front of them and form an ambuscade into which the rangers would fall. He advised his companions to go back by another route.

Captain Callaway was a dauntless fellow, and merely laughed at his friend's fears. He believed that the Indians had left the country, and that the rangers would see no more of them. Accordingly, the white men kept on their course.

They had reached the crossing at Prairie Fork, a hundred yards or more from Loutre Creek, when a terrible volley was poured into them from in front. It seemed as if the grass and bushes were on fire. Parker Hutchings, Frank McDermit, and James McMillin, who were about a hundred yards in advance with the recaptured horses, were all three instantly killed by the first volley.

Captain Callaway and the remaining rangers charged forward and plunged into the fight. They were met by a murderous fire from an ambushed foe concealed in the timber on the hill and in front. Captain Callaway's horse was killed under him, and he himself received a shot in his left arm. Another bullet struck his watch, but the timepiece turned it aside. Leaping from his dead horse, the brave captain shouted, —

"Cross the creek, charge them, and fight to the death!"

His men dashed forward and plunged into the creek. He followed them, and all were soon in the stream, which

was swollen to a considerable size by the melting snow. The water was intensely cold. Captain Callaway's wounded arm was useless, and he was compelled to swim with but one hand. When his men gained the other shore, they looked back and saw him drifting down the stream. Just then an Indian leveled a gun at him, and shot him in the back of the head. The white men saw him disappear under the water, and then turned again toward their hidden foes.

Lieutenant Riggs and the rangers fought valiantly, but the Indians outnumbered them five to one, and were all good marksmen. From the tall grass, behind trees and logs, they continued to shoot the white men, who could scarce see an enemy. The lieutenant at last ordered a retreat, after six of the rangers had fallen in the fierce conflict. The remainder recrossed Prairie Fork, and going a mile above crossed again without meeting any opposition.

Next morning they succeeded in reaching the island. Nearly every man was more or less wounded, and every horse had been struck by a bullet. The horses of the settlers were lost. Only one Indian was found dead on the battle ground, and he was buried on the prairie, near the present village of Wellsville.

The white men who had been slain in the conflict were searched out and buried. It was several days before the body of Captain Callaway was found, but it was at last discovered, caught by a bush in the stream, several hundred yards below the spot where he had been killed. The body was wrapped in blankets and buried on the side of a steep hill sloping down to Loutre Creek, and across the head of the grave was laid a flat slab, on which was engraved: "Captain James Callaway, March 7, 1815."

Callaway County was named in honor of this gallant captain of rangers.

XXII.

THE EARTHQUAKE AT NEW MADRID.

NEW MADRID was among the first settlements in Missouri. Though it was prosperous as a business village and trading post, its inhabitants were noted for their impiety. All the worst elements of a frontier river town were to be found here in this place. The residents formed a mixed class of society made up of various races and nationalities, — English, Spanish, French, Indians, and negroes. Their visitors were boatmen, hunters, trappers, and gamblers. All this went to make New Madrid what on the frontier was called "a tough place."

History says but little about the town prior to the earthquake, and that little is not to its credit. It is spoken of as the favorite resort of boatmen, who spent "their Sabbaths in drinking, gambling, and fighting." Priest and preacher went unheard, or if they were listened to at all, it was with the utmost indifference.

On December 16, 1811, many of the settlers of New Madrid observed that the atmosphere had a strange, murky appearance. Strange phenomena were not unusual on the frontier, and no one felt any great uneasiness at this, although some declared that the air was filled with the odor of sulphur.

Evening came, and many of the inhabitants retired for the night. Some of the houses were closed and dark, while in others there gleamed lights from tallow candles. There were a number of keel boats tied up along the shore. Some of them were bound for the lower country, and some were on their return trip. Masters and crews of the boats were spending the evening in drinking and gambling.

Near ten o'clock at night, there came a low rumbling of subterranean thunder which startled even those who were in deep sleep. Then came the first great shock and crash of the earthquake. Houses trembled, and people ran shrieking into the streets. Lights in the houses were extinguished, and as the night was cloudy, it was intensely dark.

A few seconds later there came a second shock, more terrible than the first. This shock, according to eyewitnesses, was "an undulating movement"; a moving up and down like the billows of the sea. Houses rocked, trees waved together, and the ground sank; while occasionally vivid flashes of lightning gleamed through the troubled clouds, rendering the darkness doubly horrible.

The shocks of this earthquake are said to have equaled in violence anything ever before known. The loss of life was not so great as might have been expected, for the country was thinly populated, and the log houses, being low, were not easily overturned.

Vast tracts of land were plunged into the Mississippi River. The graveyard at New Madrid, with all its sleeping dead, sank into the stream. Large lakes, many miles in extent, were made in a single hour, while others were drained in the same time. The whole country from the mouth of the Ohio in one direction, and to the St. Francis in another, was convulsed to such a degree as to create lakes and islands.

Trees split in the middle, lashed one with another, and tangled and .matted, inclined in every direction and at every angle. The undulations of the earth's surface were said to resemble the waves of the ocean, and they increased in elevation until the earth burst at the highest point, and great volumes of water, sand, and pit coal were discharged. Great fissures were formed where the earth had burst, and hundreds of them, some of considerable depth, still remained many years after.

Large districts were covered with white sand, which destroyed their value for agricultural purposes. Nearly the whole country, particularly that part called Little Prairie, was flooded with water. Through the forests, and in the gloom of darkest night, people fled in water up to their waists, while concussions occurring every few hours appalled all living creatures. Even the birds lost all power or disposition to fly, and sought the protection of their fellow-sufferers. As the people fled through forest and darkness, a person would occasionally sink into one of the chasms made by the earthquake, but the cries of the unfortunate brought help at once, and all who stumbled into these holes were rescued.

The force of the earthquake was much more destructive on the river than on the land. The upheaval of the river bed caused a tidal wave which for a moment changed the current of the stream. But it was only for a moment; then the waters rushed into the abyss with fearful velocity. Boats were caught in the eddying, whirling waters and destroyed, while others were thrown high and dry upon the land and left there.

An eyewitness of the terrible scene says, —

"The general impulse of the people when the shocks commenced was to fly. When the convulsions of the earth were most severe, the people were thrown down at almost every step. In the midst of those scenes of terror, all — Catholics and Protestants, praying and profane — became of one religion, and partook of one feeling. Two hundred people, speaking English, French, and Spanish, crowded. together, with pale visages and trembling forms. Mothers clasped their children to their breasts, and as soon as they could speak, all began to invoke aid from God. Even the poor, terrified horses and cattle crowded about the people for protection."

"I was in the house with my family," one man said in describing the terrible night. "Some of the children had retired, but my wife was still spinning, and I was reading a book. The first shock, which was preceded by a low rumbling sound like thunder in the bowels of the earth, threw us to the floor. Fortunately our house was not thrown down.

"'God save us, what is it?' cried my wife.

"'An earthquake. Let us fly!' I answered.

"All the children save the infant were awakened by

the first shock, and with one impulse we ran toward the door. I opened the door, and we tumbled into the street, where scores of others, screaming and wringing their hands, were assembling.

"'The babe! have you got the baby?' asked my wife.

"Then, to my horror, I discovered that our helpless infant had been left in the house. I determined to rescue it, or die in the effort.

"At this moment the second shock came — more terrific than the first. We were all thrown on the ground. It was so dark that we could see only when the pale, sickly flashes of lightning illuminated the scene. One of these flashes followed, or rather accompanied, the second shock, and by aid of it I saw the people all prostrated on the ground.

"Assisting my wife to rise, I said, —

"'Stay here with the children. Do not leave on any account, and I will go and fetch the baby!' My wife promised to obey, and I started toward the house. The earth was still shaking. I cannot describe the sensations I experienced at that time. It was as if I stood upon something that swayed from side to side, and sank and rose with irregular motions.

"I was thrown down twelve times trying to mount the piazza in front of my dwelling. At last I clutched the steps and crawled into the house, where the cries of the affrighted child could be heard. I seized it, and after many efforts succeeded in rejoining my wife. We sought a high, open spot of ground, and remained there until morning, which it seemed to us would never come.

"When morning dawned, no sun shone on us to gladden our hearts. A dense vapor arose from the seams of the earth, and hid it from view."

Little Prairie, which suffered most, contained one hundred families located in a very deep, fertile bottom. Here the earth was torn and rent by the throes of the earthquake, and some places were covered to a depth of two feet with sand. In the first paroxysm of fear, the settlers sought to escape to the hills. The depth of water, however, soon cut off their flight in that direction, and there was nothing to do but wait for the dawn of day before making any other effort to escape. When the danger was all over, every family in the settlement, except two, abandoned their homes and moved away.

The cattle and harvest at Little Prairie and New Madrid were nearly all destroyed. The people no longer dared live in houses, so they passed this winter and the succeeding one in bark wigwams and camps, like the Indians'. These were so light that if thrown down they would injure no one. A number of boats loaded with provisions were wrecked on the Mississippi above New Madrid, and their cargoes were driven down by the eddy into the mouth of the bayou which makes the harbor at the village. This accident to the boats was the salvation of the homeless villagers. Flour, beef, pork, bacon, butter, cheese, apples, in short everything that was carried down the river, floated to their ruined hamlet. The owners of boats that came safely into the bayou were so frightened that they disposed of their cargoes at nominal prices, rather than venture further down the stream.

Navigation on the Mississippi became exceedingly perilous. So changed was the river, that the oldest pilots were no longer acquainted with it. For two months, shocks continued almost daily, though no others were so severe as the two on the night of December 16. The inhabitants of New Madrid thought that the whole country below them had sunk. A great many islands in the river did sink, and new ones were raised, and the bed of the river was much changed in every respect.

After the earthquake, the country about New Madrid exhibited a melancholy aspect. There were great chasms at intervals of half or quarter of a mile, while the intervening space was covered with white sand. Trees torn up and strewn over the ground, or split in the middle as if riven by lightning, were to be seen for many miles. Congress enacted laws permitting the inhabitants of the earthquake district to locate the same amount of lands in other parts of the Territory. Certificates of claims were given to each head of a family who lived in the ruined district. But the inhabitants were mostly ignorant backwoodsmen, and shrewd and unscrupulous speculators cheated them out of their claims, so that they never received any substantial benefit from the law.

A gentleman who formerly lived in New Madrid visited it seven years after the earthquake, and wrote, —

"When I resided there, this district, formerly so level, rich, and beautiful, had the most melancholy of all aspects of decay — the tokens of former cultivation and inhabitancy, which were now mementos of desolation and desertion. Large and beautiful orchards left uninclosed, houses deserted, and deep chasms in the earth were obvious at frequent intervals. Such was the face of the country, although the people had for years become so accustomed to the frequent small shocks, which did no essential injury, that the lands were gradually rising in value, and New Madrid was slowly rebuilding with frail buildings, adapted to the apprehensions of the people."

Missouri has never since been visited by a disastrous earthquake, and the dread awakened by the convulsions at New Madrid is no longer felt.

XXIII.

MISSOURI TERRITORY.

THE region which we call Missouri was never known by this name until the year 1812. Before that time, it was known as a part of Louisiana, the Illinois District, Upper Louisiana, the District of Louisiana, and the Territory of Louisiana. No State has had more names or has changed owners more times. In 1812, it did not become the State of Missouri, but the Territory of Missouri. The Territory comprised a considerable part of Arkansas, but, on the other hand, the northern and western parts of the present State were occupied and owned by the Indians.

So many changes in rulers, names, and boundaries were the cause of many amusing incidents. One gentleman traveling through the Territory met another from the Boones Lick country, and asked him where he lived; and the latter replied, —

"I lived in the Illinois District yesterday, but we change names and rulers so often that I would not venture to say where I live now, or to what country I belong."

On June 4, 1812, Missouri Territory was organized by Congress, with a governor, a legislative council, and a house of representatives. The governor was appointed by the President of the United States, and had the power of absolute veto. Only one man was ever appointed to the office — William Clark, one of the commanders of the Lewis and Clark expedition. His term as governor did not begin till 1813, but it lasted until Missouri became a State, in 1821. In organizing the Territory of Missouri, it was divided into five counties: St. Charles, St. Louis, Ste. Genevieve, Cape Girardeau, and New Madrid. Each of these counties elected members to the Territorial House of Representatives, and together they sent one delegate to Congress. The Legislative Council was composed of nine men, selected by the President from a list of eighteen who were chosen by the House of Representatives.

The capital of Missouri was St. Louis, and here, in due course, her first Territorial Legislature met. The members were, for the most part, men with little or no experience in lawmaking. It is said that when they had assembled, one member arose and asked, —

"What did we come here for?"

If the members were ignorant of their duties, the people were still more so.

"What's that crowd doing?" asked a hunter who had just entered the city.

"That's the Legislature."

"What's a Legislature?"

It was explained to him that a Legislature was an assembly of men who met to make laws for the people.

"We don't want any laws," declared the hunter. "We won't have any laws, and the best thing we can do is to drive the Legislature out of town."

But the suggestion did not meet with favor, and the legislators were permitted to continue their business uninterrupted. They proceeded first to enact a law regulating a system of weights and measures. They created the office of sheriff in each county, and enacted a law for taking the census of the Territory. Permanent seats of justice, or county seats, were located, and provision was made for the compensation of all Territorial and county officers.

Laws were passed prohibiting crimes, and providing for the punishment of the offenders. Among the early acts, also, was the granting of a charter to the first bank in Missouri — the Bank of St. Louis.

People soon began to appreciate the work of the lawmakers, and there was a remarkable change for the better in the morals of the inhabitants. At the second session of the Legislature, laws were enacted to regulate elections, and to suppress vice and immorality on the Sabbath. The offices of Territorial treasurer, auditor, and county surveyor were established, and laws were passed for the improvement of public roads.

The Territory filled up rapidly, and new counties were soon formed.

In 1816–17, among other acts of the Legislature, was one to encourage the "killing of wolves, panthers, and wild cats." A reward of five dollars was offered for the scalp of every one of these animals that was killed. The scalp was the skin on the top of the head, including the two ears. Scalps were taken to the clerks of the county courts, who gave an order on the treasury for five dollars for each one.

This law met with great favor among hunters and trappers. They concluded that lawmakers were of some use after all, and there was no more talk of running them out of town. Through all the various changes of State government since the early days of Missouri, the "wolf-scalp law," as it is known, has remained on the statute books, subject to only slight modifications.

For some time after the formation of the Territory, the Boones Lick country attracted more immigrants than did any other part of Missouri. The town now known as Old Franklin, situated two miles from the present town of Franklin, was laid out in 1816, in what was called Coopers Bottom, opposite the present city of Boonville.

Franklin, being in the center of the salt-making district, soon became a thrifty village. About this time a brisk trade between Missouri and Santa Fé, New Mexico, was opened up. It consisted of an exchange of furs, salt, and the other products of Missouri, for coffee, silver, and wool. The trade was known as the Santa Fé trade, and the route pursued by the traders was for many years called the old Santa Fé trail.

At first the goods were carried across the country on the backs of pack horses and mules, but after a time wagons were used in place of them. These wagons, because of their sloping beds, and great white covers, were called "prairie schooners," and they were usually drawn by eight or ten horses or oxen.

The Santa Fé trade was attended with great toil and danger, so the traders usually traveled in large wagon trains for mutual protection. Sometimes one train contained as many as fifty wagons. Before starting on one of these journeys, officers were elected, and every one was obliged to obey them. There was a captain of the wagon train, who had supreme command. Then there was a wagon master, who had control of all the wagons, and who had authority to

condemn or abandon any, if the safety of the train required it. A guide was employed who possessed a perfect knowledge of the trail, and of the Indians through whose country it passed, or with whom the party was liable to come into contact.

Franklin was the starting point for these fleets of prairie schooners. The increase of this town in wealth and commerce during the brisk days of the Santa Fé trade, and of the Boones Lick salt works, was wonderful. It was here that the first newspaper west of St.

Louis was established. It was started by Nathaniel Patton in April, 1819, and was called the *Missouri Intelligencer*.

In May, 1819, the steamboat "Independence," commanded by Captain Nelson, left St. Louis and began the first trip ever made by any steamer on the Missouri River. As it entered the turbid waters of the great stream, all the passengers on board felt that this trial trip was not without danger.

The large paddle wheels sent the waves with great force against the sandy banks. Occasionally a rushing sound was heard, a violent splash, and great masses of the sandy bank would fall into the stream. To the timid and inexperienced, this was a dangerous sign; but the brave captain steadily held his course, and at the end of twelve days reached the village of Franklin, his destination.

All the town turned out to greet the arrival of the first steamboat at Franklin. But this was only the beginning of navigation on the Missouri, and until railroads supplanted water transportation, the Missouri River was the great thoroughfare by which the interior of the State was reached.

XXIV.

FANATICAL PILGRIMS.

AMONG the many curious people who settled in Missouri during the Territorial days, was a class of religious fanatics known in history as the Fanatical Pilgrims. They came to Missouri in the year 1817, and for some time their influence was strongly felt in that part of the Territory in which they had settled.

This strange society was heard of first in Lower Canada. A few enthusiastic people began to discuss the deadness and unworthiness of all religious bodies, and grew anxious to separate themselves from all church organizations, in order to form a more perfect society. Others soon caught the enthusiasm, and hastened to join the new movement.

What induced these people to start out on a pilgrimage to the southwest is not positively known. Some think that it came about by misinterpreting the text, "sell whatsoever thou hast, give to the poor, . . . and follow me." However that may be, they sold their earthly possessions, or put them into a common stock, and began their pilgrimage.

They had a leader whom they called their prophet. Whether he was an impostor or was insane, it is impossible to determine. They traveled through Vermont and New York, gathering recruits all along their route. When questioned as to where they were going, they declared that there was a New Jerusalem far to the southwest, and that they were journeying there to make it their home.

They arrived at New Madrid in boats, and walked ashore in Indian file; the old men in front, and the women and children in the rear. As they walked, they chanted a kind of a hymn, the burden of which was, —

"Praise God! Praise God!"

At New Madrid they stopped and organized their society. They had about eight or ten thousand dollars' worth of property, which was held in common. The prophet was their ruler, spiritual and temporal. He had visions at night, which he expounded in the morning, and by these he determined whether they should stop or go on, whether the journey should be by land or water, — in short, everything was settled by immediate inspiration.

Their food was mush and milk prepared in a trough; and it is said that they stood up in rows by it, and sucked what they wanted through hollow reeds or perforated cornstalks. They imposed terrible penalties on those violating the law of God, as they interpreted it. In some respects they were very much like the Mormons, who followed about two decades later; but they differed from the later sect in being indolent and filthy, for the Mormons were usually clean and industrious. Among other peculiarities, the Fanatical Pilgrims affected a ragged dress in which were different stripes, like those of the convicts in penitentiaries. They also wore caps made of the same striped material.

So formidable a band of ragged pilgrims, marching in perfect order and chanting with a peculiar twang the short phrase, " Praise God! Praise God! " had in it something imposing to people like those in Missouri.

Especially was this the case in New Madrid, where the inhabitants had not yet recovered from the unnatural dread occasioned by the earthquake. The coming of this strange company into a house caused the people a thrill of alarm. Food lost its savor while they were calling upon the inhabitants, standing with eyes turned upward, as motionless as statues, and chanting, —

"Praise God! Fast and pray!" Small children cried with fright at sight of these people, and hid themselves from view.

At New Madrid, two of the most distinguished pilgrims determined to leave the band. Their intentions were found out, and they were placed in confinement under a guard; but at last they succeeded in making their escape. One of them was an accomplished lady, whose overwrought imagination had been carried away by the imposing rites of the pilgrims; and soon after her escape she died from the starvation and hardships she had endured while with them.

The band finally settled on Pilgrims Island, opposite Little Prairie, where they remained a long time. Here the most senseless, useless, and wicked rites were practiced. In accordance with his own interpretation of the text, "Let the dead bury their dead," the prophet refused to allow his people to make any burials, and the bones of the dead pilgrims were left to bleach in the sun.

This sect, which at one time numbered hundreds, finally began to dwindle away. Evil-minded boatmen landed on the island and robbed them, for their religion would not permit them to defend themselves. Many made their escape from the island, and scattered over the southern part of Missouri, wiser and better people.

The sheriff of New Madrid was once informed that there were children among these fanatics, starving for want of food; so he loaded a boat with provisions, and set out for the island with three or four deputies.

On reaching the place he was met by the tall, gaunt prophet, hollow-eyed, and staring like a lunatic.

"Who are ye?" he demanded.

"I am the sheriff of New Madrid."

"What seek ye here? This is the land of the holy, and we have no need of sheriffs."

The officer then explained that he had brought a boat load of provisions for the starving children. At this intelligence, the little ones, to the number of two or three score, began to press forward, eager to get the food. It was a sad sight. Their little faces were pinched with hunger, and their forms were so emaciated that they were like living skeletons.

When the prophet learned the mission of the sheriff, he cried, —

"Away with your food. We are commanded to fast and pray!"

He shrieked, and waved his long, bony arms in the air; and his gaunt form looked so like a specter that for a moment the sheriff was filled with awe. But the sight of the starving children, crowding forward and begging for bread, aroused the officer to a sense of his duty. He started toward the prophet, saying, —

"I have come with food for the children. It is my duty to give it to them, and you must not interfere."

Turning to the little ones, the prophet cried, —

"Take no food!" In such awe was this man held, that the starving children shrank away from the food which they were craving.

"You shall not starve those children," declared the sheriff.

"Better that their bodies perish than that their souls should be cast into hell fire."

The sheriff, finding explanation and reasoning useless, determined to resort to force.

"I have brought the children something to eat, and I shall give it to them," he declared. "Do not hinder me."

He then ordered the men to bring the food on shore and distribute it among the little ones. The prophet gave utterance to a wild cry, and a dozen of his followers, gaunt, ragged, and haggard as himself, came to his side.

The sheriff drew his sword, and, advancing toward them, cried, —

"Stand back, insane wretches! I shall feed those children, if I have to kill you."

The gleam of his sword, the flash of his determined eye, and his threatening manner frightened the prophet and his followers. They fell back, and the children pressed forward and ravenously devoured the food which had been brought for them.

The older people could be induced to eat but little, for the prophet declared that God's wrath would fall upon all who touched the food.

Many of the pilgrims, cured of their fanaticism, left the island and settled in various parts of Missouri. Dwindled to an insignificant number, the band finally removed to Arkansas, where their leaders died; and the remainder soon gave up the folly of such a life, and became more sensible and consistent Christians.

XXV.

THE EARLY LAWYER.

OUTSIDE of the towns, some of which were rapidly becoming cities, there was very little litigation in Missouri during the Territorial days. In the first place, property was seldom valuable enough to go to law about; and, besides this, there was a rude honesty and sense of justice among the pioneers, which impelled them to obey the golden rule.

Their differences were settled more frequently by arbitration than by law. The plan of arbitration was very simple. Each party would choose a neighbor, and these two would choose a third; the committee of three would meet, hear both sides, and then go to a log and sit down to discuss the question in dispute. When a decision was reached, they called the interested parties and announced their award, — generally more just than the decision of a court, — and the parties usually accepted it in silence.

If, however, they were still disposed to disagree and be unneighborly, some of the pioneers would get them together and lecture them on the "unreasonableness of their differences," and the bad effect it had on the "settlement;" and often the parties would be thus induced to "make up." When they "made up," they shook hands in the presence of the committee, and such a settlement was usually lasting.

Some of the early justices of the peace, or magistrates, and even judges of the circuit courts were very ignorant of the law. Their decisions were based on their ideas of justice and their strong common sense. Many amusing stories are told of these early magistrates, which illustrate the character of the early inhabitants of the State, as well as that of their judicial proceedings.

A man named Brown, a blacksmith by trade, was elected justice of the peace. He was a man of some qualifications, as he was able to write, and could read fairly well in the New Testament, the only book he had; but Brown knew nothing of law, or of legal proceedings.

The first case that he had was a difficult one. A man named Nelson came to him and complained of being robbed. Mr. Nelson knew the thief, but to recover the property was impossible, as it had been destroyed. Nelson had a neighbor named Evans. Mr. Evans had a dog named Tray, and this dog was the thief that had robbed Mr. Nelson. During the silent hours of the night, Tray, with malice aforethought, had entered Mr. Nelson's smokehouse and had stolen and carried away three bacon hams.

Mr. Evans, the owner of Tray, had no part in the theft, as he was sound asleep, and so, of course, he was not responsible. After giving the matter due consideration, and consulting with disinterested parties, the new magistrate issued a warrant for Tray. The constable arrested the dog, and brought him before the magistrate. The blacksmith's shop was converted into a court of justice.

As the defendant was unable to speak for himself, the magistrate ordered the constable to summon a jury to try the case. The jury was duly impaneled and sworn, and a number of witnesses were then examined. The testimony brought out against Tray was very damaging.

All the while the defendant lay stretched out on the bare earth, his nose between his fore paws, perfectly unconcerned. The jury were an hour making their verdict. The decision was that the dog should be whipped.

"But how about the costs?" asked the magistrate.

"The constable is to pay the costs," answered the foreman of the jury, gravely. The constable objected, but no appeal was taken, and, as no one knew how much the costs were, they were never collected. Poor Tray was tied to a tree, and received the full penalty of the sentence; but it is certain that he never knew why he got that flogging.

* * * * * * * *

Dr. Willis P. King, in his "Stories of a Country Doctor," relates an incident which illustrates some of the characteristics of these early justices.

"In the 'good old days,' a case was being tried before a justice of the peace. The litigants had had difficulties growing out of the close proximity of their farms. Cross fences, breachy cattle, and other such matters had finally brought them into court to settle their disputes. They were very bitter against each other, and as the trial progressed they grew more and more so, until at last they began to hurl invectives at each other right before the seat of justice. Finally they began to 'talk fight' and one of them said, —

"'If you can whip me, you can settle this your own way.'

"The other responded with a like statement, and at it they went. They were soon down on the floor, rolling and tumbling, biting and gouging, after the fashion of those days. The jury arose to their feet, and everything was excitement and confusion. Several men shouted, —

"'Don't let 'em fight! Part 'em! Part 'em!'

"The justice sprang into the midst of the surging crowd, but instead of 'commanding the peace,' as was his duty, yelled out, —

"'Let 'em alone, men; let 'em fight it out; if they can settle it that way, it will save the costs.'"

For judicial purposes, the Territory was divided into judicial circuits, just as it is to-day. The circuits of that time were very extensive. A county was about as large then as a Congressional district is now, but it required several counties to make a circuit. Men having business in court were sometimes compelled to travel from thirty to one hundred miles to reach the place where the judge was to sit.

Travel was nearly altogether on horseback. Judge and lawyers went together from town to town, or "rode the circuit," as it was called. Their journeys were often through vast forests, or across prairies with only a bridle path to follow. Their books and legal papers were carried in saddlebags. To enliven such a tour through the boundless forest, the lawyers, clients, and judges would relate anecdotes and sketches of adventure.

If there happened to be one along who had some musical ability, — and such a one could usually be found in the party, — he would unpack a flute or fiddle from his saddlebags, and strike up the melody of some popular air or song of the time, in which the company would often join with a hearty chorus. There were stopping places along the way, usually some lonely cabin, where the frontiersman entertained his guests as best he could. Often eight or ten men would spend the night in a house which had but a single room. The best bed or couch was given to the judge, and if there were others they were occupied by the lawyers. If there were not enough beds, some of the men slept on the floor or in the barn loft.

* * * * * * * *

In those days men avoided going to law, for it was thought a disgrace to have "been in court." A man who was continually suing or being sued was considered a meddlesome, quarrelsome fellow, and no one wanted to have any dealings with him.

There was a young farmer named Skinner living on the frontier, who was usually a quiet, mild fellow; but one day he became intoxicated at a logrolling, and was the aggressor in a fist fight. He was arrested and taken before a justice of the peace, where he gave bail for his appearance at circuit court.

Skinner hated courts and lawyers, for he regarded the latter as meddlesome and unprincipled. He was indicted by the grand jury; and his father-in-law, without his knowledge, employed an attorney to defend him at his trial.

When the case of the "State vs. Skinner" was called, the lawyer answered that he appeared for the defendant.

"No he don't, Judge," cried Skinner, leaping to his feet. "I don't want any lawyer. I'd rather go to jail than have anything to do with one of those fellows."

"What are you going to do with your case?" asked the judge.

"Give me a clearance of that bond, and I don't care what you do with the case."

The judge asked what the man meant by "a clearance of the bond," and was informed by the defendant that he had given bond for his appearance at court, and that he wanted his sureties released.

The judge said he must go on trial, and asked him where his lawyer was.

"Here's my lawyer," Skinner answered, tapping his breast. A jury was impaneled; Skinner defended his own cause, much to the amusement of all; and he secured an acquittal.

Some of the entries to be found in the dockets kept by the early justices of the peace are amusing. The following is a literal transcript of a judgment rendered by one:—

PETE LANTZ Plf.
vs
ABE WOLF Deft
Before W. W. M — J. P.

August 16, 1822.
Plantiff sued Defendant on a plane not of hand. Constable surved papers. Sot for trial August 27th. Now comes Abe Wolf and wants a jury, and i giv it to him. Judgement for lantz for a yerling steer. Abe Wolf wants to appeal, the justis cant see it.

During the thirties, there lived a lawyer in Boonville who was a terror to witnesses on cross-examination. He was original, witty, tyrannical, sarcastic, and abusive in his addresses to juries. Strong men grew speechless when he opened fire on them.

A Mr. B., an excellent old farmer, found himself at last dragged into a lawsuit in spite of his aversion to courts. Being unaccustomed to the rigid cross-examination of lawyers, he became confused in some of his statements.

The lawyer took advantage of this to abuse him unmercifully before the jury. Mr. B. had a son named John, a great, strapping fellow of nineteen. The lawyer's abuse became unbearable, and before John was hardly aware of what he was about, he leaped to his feet and knocked the lawyer down.

John was at once arrested, and fined fifty dollars for contempt of court. His father paid the fine. The lawyer, having washed and dressed his wounds, resumed his ungentlemanly and uncalled-for assault on the old man's character. The farmer looked at his son, and said, —

"Well, John, I've got a little more money."

John needed no second hint, but sprang at the attorney. That gentleman, seeing his danger, leaped from an open window and ran down the street at full speed, pursued by John, while the jury applauded. The lawyer's dread of the old man's son, and his own long legs, saved him from a severe beating, but he lost his case. The jury gave a verdict in favor of the man he had abused.

XXVI.[1]

THOMAS H. BENTON.

ON August 10, 1821, Missouri was declared a State. The proposition to admit this Territory into the Union gave rise to a long and bitter debate in Congress, as to whether it should be admitted as a free or as a slave State. At last the question was settled by a compromise which was brought about mainly through the efforts of Henry Clay. A bill was passed admitting Missouri as a slave State, but prohibiting slavery in all other States that should be admitted to the Union, north of latitude thirty-six degrees and thirty minutes. This was the "Missouri Compromise."

Missouri's first State election was held in 1820, before she was formally admitted. Alexander McNair was chosen as the first governor. Other State officers, including members of the State Senate and House of Representatives, were also chosen. The people of the State elected their own representatives to Congress, but the two United States senators had to be chosen by the Legislature or General Assembly, as the legislative branch of the State government was called. David Barton was made one senator without opposition; but over the second senatorship there arose a bitter contest.

[1] The material for this chapter is partly from Switzler's "History of Missouri."

About the year 1815 there came to Missouri, from Tennessee, a man who had already distinguished himself as a lawyer and statesman, Thomas H. Benton. He was a man of great ability, but possessed strong prejudices. His friends loved him, and his enemies hated him. Benton was ambitious to put himself forward as a candidate for United States senator, and the announcement of his intention roused his foes and friends to the highest pitch of excitement. The rivals of Benton for the office were Judge John B. C. Lucas, Henry Elliott, John R. Jones, and Nathaniel Cook. His most formidable opponent was Judge Lucas, a man who was honorable and popular, and who had proved himself a faithful public officer. Judge Lucas was not only a political, but also a personal enemy of Colonel Benton; for only three years before, his son, Charles Lucas, had been killed by Benton in a duel.

Thomas H. Benton.

The General Assembly met at the Missouri Hotel, corner of Main and Morgan streets, in St. Louis, September 19, 1820, for the purpose of electing United States senators. When it became known that Benton was an aspirant for the office, he met with the bitterest opposition that the murdered man's father could arouse; yet dueling in those days was not thought to be criminal, but honorable, and Benton had many warm friends.

After the unanimous election of the first senator, the assembly proceeded to ballot for the other; but as no one of the candidates received a majority of the votes, there was no choice. The members of the Legislature voted again and again, day after day, with always a similar result. The excitement which was aroused has never been equaled in any other election in the State. The assembly found itself unable to come to any decision. Mr. Barton having been already selected, it was thought best to consult his wishes as to which man he would prefer to have for his colleague; and he chose Benton. This added to the strength of the latter, but from the great opposition to him it still seemed impossible to elect him.

Judge Lucas, powerful and influential, rallied all his personal friends to his support, and urged them to remain steadfast in their opposition to his rival; and the other candidates, though losing part of their support, still remained in the contest.

One of the men who supported neither Lucas nor Benton was Marie Le Duc, a Frenchman of considerable prominence. He lived in St. Louis, and had been the secretary and assistant of Delassus, the last Spanish lieutenant governor. Le Duc was strongly opposed to Benton's election, and had publicly vowed to cut off his right hand before it should ever cast a vote for him.

Nevertheless, the friends of Benton determined to win Le Duc over to their side; for it seemed to be their only chance of gaining the one vote now lacking for a majority. Fortunately for Benton, some of his friends had a powerful influence over Le Duc. Among them was Colonel Auguste Chouteau, one of the founders of St. Louis, and long a prominent figure in its history.

The pet idea of Le Duc was to secure from Congress the confirmation of the French and Spanish land claims. Knowing this, the shrewd politicians assailed his weakest point. They assured him that the race lay between Benton and Lucas, and that the senator chosen would surely decide the fate of the land grants; for Benton was in favor of confirming them, while Lucas wanted them declared invalid. Le Duc spent most of one night arguing with Benton's friends, and ended by consenting to act with them.

But even now there was still trouble, for the friends of Benton remembered that one of their number was dangerously sick, and his vote was necessary for their victory. This member was Daniel Ralls, for whom Ralls County was afterwards named. It was necessary to move quickly, for it was feared that Ralls might die. Without disclosing their plans, Benton's friends in the assembly hastened to have another vote called for. The room occupied by Mr. Ralls was upstairs in the hotel where the Legisla-

ture met, but that day he was too sick to sit in a chair, and almost too weak to stir. Therefore, at the proper time, four negroes carried him into the assembly room just as he lay on his bed. When his name was called, he voted for Thomas H. Benton; and this vote elected Benton to the United States Senate, of which he was a member for thirty years.

Although there was much in the personal character of Benton which one cannot admire, yet he was an able statesman of his day, and his influence was long felt in Missouri. His wisdom and patriotism are unquestionable. The darkest stain on his character was the killing of young Lucas, and this, it is said, he never ceased to regret.

Mr. Ralls died a few days after the election of Benton. That vote was his last official act.

XXVII.

SOME CUSTOMS AND PEOPLE OF THE PAST.

PEOPLE who have always lived in comfortable homes in a city or village, or even on a farm, cannot realize the difficulties and hardships of the pioneer in a new country. The early immigrant in Missouri found a land with rich soil, pure water, beautiful prairies, and noble forests; but what were all these, compared with a comfortable home?

It required years of toil to make a home with even a few comforts. The pioneer had to cut down great trees, and build himself a house, or rather a cabin, which was usually inferior to the ordinary cow shed of the present time. He had to turn up the soil with a poor plow, and sometimes even dig it up with a grubbing hoe, in order to get the hazel roots out. He had to split rails, make fences, build barns and bridges, and perhaps go a hundred miles to mill. Everything had to be done at a sacrifice of time and labor which would be appalling to one of the present age. After all his toil, if his farm should yield more than he could use, his produce became a burden on his hands, unless enough newcomers came in to help him consume it. Such a thing as a market for surplus production was out of the question.

After Missouri became a State, the pioneer was too far advanced to dress wholly in buckskin, like the settlers who preceded him. The early Missourian therefore raised sheep and grew flax; and his wife and daughters had to spin, dye, warp, and weave, and make all the clothing for the family, — woolen for winter, and linen for summer wear.

Though the Indians had been driven from his immediate neighborhood, the Missouri farmer still had enemies. These were the bears, minks, raccoons, crows, blackbirds, and blue jays, which made raids on his pigpens, henroosts, and cornfields.

If the streams became swollen so that he could not go to mill, and the family were out of bread, they had to resort to "gritting."

The "gritter" was made from a piece of tin, usually an old coffeepot flattened out. This was first perforated all over with a nail, all the perforations being made from the same side, so that the opposite surface was made very rough. The tin was then bent and nailed to a board, with the rough, convex side outward.

If the corn was hard, it was boiled until soft enough to be gritted. If it was new corn, just "out of the roasting ear," or if it had "just passed the milk," it did not need to be boiled. The person who did the work sat down and put one end of the gritter in a big wooden tray, and the other end between his knees. Then, grasping the ear of corn by the ends, he rubbed it over the rough surface, cutting off fine particles of meal, which fell into the tray. The meal was then sifted and made into corn bread in the usual way.

"Lye hominy" was another homemade luxury, which may still be found in some parts of the State. It often took the place of bread, and frequently all the food in the house was pork and hominy. This gave rise to the expression "hog and hominy," which in the early days of the State was a synonym for food.

It was impossible to get many nails, and hence some way had to be devised for doing without them. The boards that covered the houses and other buildings were laid on in the usual way, and then weighted down with poles, which were held in position by wooden pins. The man who owned an auger, a drawing knife, a handsaw, and a chisel was considered a person of note.

After years and years of such toil and privation, comforts came. Cultivation took the wild nature out of the soil; better houses succeeded the cabins; stock grew and multiplied; mills and towns came nearer; and schoolhouses became more plentiful, and teachers better prepared for their business.

* * * * * * * *

A shiftless class of humanity always appears in the second stage of civilization in a new country. Missouri was no exception to this rule, and such a class was found within her borders about the time that the Indians were driven out. These people were called "branch-water men," and some of them may yet be found in the wildest parts of the State. The "branch-water man" is a product peculiar to the West. He is never met with in the East, and no history of Europe mentions him. He is usually descended from a long line of "branch-water" ancestry. He is tall, lank, and stoop-shouldered, and has that peculiar listless air of repose which Washington Irving tells us pervades Sleepy Hollow. Yet he is a nomadic personage. He never has a home, and never wants one, unless he can sell it and "move." He is the American gypsy, without the ability to barter and trade, but he is nearly always honest and inoffensive.

The branch-water man lives back of some other man's farm, and drinks branch water in preference to digging a well; because to dig a well would cost him some exertion, and he is an enemy to anything like labor. One can always tell this man by his dog and his wagon. Dr. King thus describes the dog:—

"This man's dog is a mongrel. He is a mixture of all the dogs of the meaner kind that you ever saw. He is generally a yellow dog, and has a long body, short legs, and a bushy tail. As said before, he is a mixture of many breeds of dogs; but he is most of all 'branch-water man's dog.' When you see that kind of a dog on the streets of a country town, you can find the master by going around to the wood yard and picking out the man with the smallest, trashiest, and meanest load of stove wood in the lot."

His wagon is always ancient, the sides showing great indentations made by the teeth of a horse. It is a squeaky old affair which threatens every moment to fall into ruins. The tires are usually too large for the wheels, and are held on with hickory withes.

The team that pulls it usually consists of a big horse and a small mule, or a small horse and a big mule, both old, feeble, and thin in flesh. One usually has a big knee, and the other a crooked leg, spring halt, or some other bodily infirmity. If the two beasts possess one eye between them, they are lucky.

The branch-water man seldom remains longer than one season in a place. Then he puts his wife and several children into the old creaky wagon, puts out the fire, whistles to his dog, and is ready to move. The creaky old wagon can contain not only his numerous family, but all his household effects as well.

* * * * * * * *

The young people who grew up in the days of toil and hardship had their enjoyment, just as the young people do now. The old-time dances and "frolics," as they were called, are still remembered with pleasure by some of the older residents of the State.

All the young people did not dance in those days. Some had religious scruples against it. The early pioneer preachers forbade it as wicked, and those dances caused no end of trouble and church trials. But often a young convert, at the sound of the fiddle, could not resist the temptation, and before he or she was hardly aware of it, was "on the floor."

A substitute for this sort of amusement which was tolerated by the church members was the "social party," "play party," or, as they were sometimes called, "kissing bees." At these, such games as "Weevilly Wheat," "Sister Phœby," "We're Marching down to Old Quebec," and "King William," were played for the amusement of the young people.

If it was announced that there was to be a dance, "frolic," or "kissing bee" at a house on a certain night, soon after dark the young people would begin to arrive. They came from all parts of the country,

some on foot, some on horseback, and a few, who came from a distance, in wagons.

The dancing was usually of the rudest sort. The fiddler sawed away on his cracked instrument all night long on such airs as "Old Dan Tucker," "Zip Coon,"

"Natches under the Hill," "Rickets," "Fisher's Hornpipe," "Sailor's Hornpipe," "Run, Nigger, Run," "Soap Suds," "Great Big Tater in the Sandy Land," and others of like character. When not engaged in dancing or talking with the girls, the young men usually discussed farming, logging, or clearing off the forest and plowing the ground.

* * * * * * * *

In every settlement there were enough pious people to get together and found a church. At first the meetings were held in the people's houses, but after a while in schoolhouses; and then, as the population became more dense, a log church was erected. A traveling preacher, usually called a "circuit rider," was engaged to come and preach to the people once a month, or maybe only once in every two months.

Several years later, when the congregation became larger and had more money, a Sunday school was organized. A superintendent was chosen, and teachers volunteered to instruct the children. Little boys and girls, barefooted and dressed in homespun, were at these schools every Sunday, and in them many laid the foundation of an excellent education.

Though the people on the frontier endured much, they were free from many annoyances which civilization brings, and perhaps, on the whole, enjoyed life as much as their more refined descendants.

XXVIII.

THE NEW CAPITAL.

ST. LOUIS was the center of commerce in Missouri, but so many settlements had sprung up in the interior that it was not a convenient point for the capital of the State. Members of the Legislature complained that they had too great a distance to travel.

"Why, I have to start a month before I'm elected, to reach the capital in time for the opening of the Legislature," said one member, who lived far in the interior.

In 1821 the capital was changed to St. Charles, but even this location was not sufficiently central. Immigrants were pushing out upon the broad prairies and into the deep forests, and districts which were a wilderness but a short time before were rapidly being filled with frontiersmen's cabins. Farmers, traders, and salt makers had settled all over the Boones Lick country.

The members of the Legislature declared that they must have a new capital; and it was decided to select some place which was favorable in other respects, and at the same time would be easy of access to the members from the different parts of the State.

Five commissioners were appointed to choose the site. They were John Thornton of Howard County, Robert Gray Watson of New Madrid County, John B.-

White of Pike County, James Logan of Wayne County, and Jesse B. Boone of Montgomery County.

The revised constitution of the State required that the capital be located on the Missouri River within forty miles of the mouth of the Osage. The commissioners set out on their expedition, went up to the mouth of the Osage, and proceeded to inspect the country along the shores of the Missouri.

The settlers in that part of the State were often puzzled to know what the committeemen were doing.

"Say, are you fellows hunting salt or bee trees?" asked an old hunter, when he came upon them.

"We are hunting for a location for the capital," answered one of the committeemen.

The old man gazed at them for a moment in open-mouthed astonishment. He was ashamed to display his ignorance by asking for an explanation, and yet was unable to fathom the meaning of the answer. After a moment's silence, he took his gun from his shoulder, and, shaking his head, said, —

"There's no such beast in these woods."

The committeemen then explained that they were seeking a location for the State buildings, including a prison. This did not please the old hunter.

"We don't want them," he said. "What do we want with prisons? I came here to be free, and as long as you keep away with your laws and prisons I shall be. We don't do anything here to go to prison for, and if you'll keep away with them, we'll all get along first rate."

The commissioners did not waste much time arguing with this man, whose ideas of civilization were so different from their own.

After examining many locations, they decided upon the spot where Jefferson City now stands. The land was surveyed, and the commissioners returned to St. Charles and made their report, which was approved by the governor and the General Assembly.

In 1822, men were sent out to survey the new town and lay it out in lots. It was called Jefferson City in honor of Thomas Jefferson, the third President of the United States.

Work was immediately begun upon the State building, and a village soon sprang up about it. The capitol was erected on the four sections of land donated to Missouri by the United States government. It was made of brick, and stood on precisely the same site as that on which the governor's mansion now stands. It was large enough to meet the needs of the State, but it was destroyed by fire in 1837; and the oldest portion of the present capitol was erected in the next year.

During the year 1825, while the first building was in course of construction, Marquis de Lafayette, then visiting the United States, honored Missouri with his presence. He was received at St. Louis with every demonstration of joy and gratitude, and as much patriotism was displayed as if Missouri had been one of the original thirteen colonies.

Next year (in 1826), the new State building was far enough advanced for the Legislature to meet at the new capital. It was the fourth meeting of this body since Missouri had become a State. Jefferson City was at this time only a little backwoods village, and most of the buildings were of logs. Hotel accommodations were poor, and when the legislators met it was difficult to provide for them.

There is a story told of an enterprising landlord who established a unique hotel in the new capital. His building was a board structure, one story in height and without a floor. The office occupied the front part of the building, and the dining room and kitchen, the rear. A newly elected member of the Legislature asked if he could be provided here with board and lodging.

"Certainly," answered the landlord. "That is what I am here for."

"Have you a comfortable room and bed?"

"Yes, sir, plenty of good rooms and beds. I will give you number fifteen."

The member, who could see nothing but the front office and the kitchen, sat until supper was announced, puzzling his brain to locate room number fifteen.

Soon after the meal, he expressed a wish to retire; and the landlord, seizing a tallow candle, led him to an open space of ground in the rear of his board house. Here a row of tents had been pitched, and before one of them was stuck a pine board on which was rudely painted, "No. 15." Inside the tent was a rude cot, on which the legislator reposed.

The first capitol was erected at a cost of twenty-five thousand dollars. It was a simple two-story structure, without any architectural ornamentation. The House of Representatives met on the lower floor, while the Senate was "upstairs." Many anecdotes are told of

the mistakes of members at the first meeting in the new building. It is said that one member of the House of Representatives took his credentials to the clerk of the Senate.

"This does not belong here," said the clerk. "You must take this to the lower house."

"Where is that?"

"Downstairs."

"Why, I saw those fellows down there," said the member, "but I thought it was a grocery."

XXIX.

THE BIG NECK WAR.—THE PLATTE PURCHASE.

DOWN to the year 1824, the extreme northern part of Missouri, or what now comprises the three northern tiers of counties, was unsettled by white men, and was claimed by the Iowa Indians. In that year, a delegation of chiefs and warriors, headed by White Cloud, went to Washington with General William Clark, ex-governor of Missouri. Here a treaty was made, by the terms of which the Indians ceded to the whites all their lands in 'Missouri—amounting to about two million acres. In return for this, they were to receive five hundred dollars a year for ten years: as was usually the case with Indian treaties, advantage was taken of savage ignorance.

The counties of Platte, Buchanan, Andrew, Holt, Atchison, and Nodaway were not at that time a part of Missouri; for, as we shall soon see, they were acquired by the Platte purchase in 1837. In 1824, this district was reserved for the Indians, and they were to remove to it.

Among the Indians who took part in this treaty was a celebrated brave called, in English, Big Neck. He was not an hereditary chief, but a bold warrior who by his ability had raised himself to the leadership of a band in his tribe. He was very ambitious, and was exceedingly jealous of the hereditary chiefs. With a band of about sixty, he separated himself from the others, and, disregarding the authority of the chiefs, roamed about the country wherever he pleased.

His favorite hunting grounds were the vast tracts of land drained by the Chariton and Grand rivers in northern Missouri. The Chariton was abundantly supplied with fish, while deer and elk in great numbers roamed over the prairies and through the woods of what is now included in Adair, Macon, Schuyler, and Putnam counties. Big Neck claimed that he did not comprehend the treaty of 1824, by which he relinquished his lands in Missouri. He said it was his understanding, when he signed the treaty, that he and his band were to be allowed to live along the Chariton River for ten years. He was told he must rejoin his tribe, and live under the authority of his tribal chief, Mahakah. This he refused to do, and for two years made his home on the Chariton.

In 1828, most of the Indians having moved according to the treaty, settlements were made along the Chariton River; and a year later, the county of Randolph was formed, which included a large part of north Missouri. One of the settlements, known as the "Cabins of the White Folks," was made near the present site of Kirksville; it did not contain more than a dozen families. Prior to this, there had been some cattle grazers in the Chariton country, and it had also become a noted resort for bee hunters.

In July, 1829, Big Neck and his band of sixty Indians came down from the north, and encamped on the Chariton about nine miles northwest of the Cabins of the White Folks. One day, some of these Indians, while hunting along the Chariton bottom, came upon a drove of hogs belonging to the white men, and their dogs killed several.

Next day three bold frontiersmen, Isaac Gross, John Cain, and Jim Myers, visited Big Neck at his camp, and not only protested against the conduct of the Indians, but insisted that they must leave Missouri.

"This country now belongs to us," said the white men, "and you must leave it. You signed away your right to it, and now you must pay us for the hogs you have killed, go away, and never come back again."

"I did not sign the treaty," Big Neck defiantly replied. "I have come back here to live, and you must take your cattle and go away; or, if you want to fight, come on!" His warriors, with loaded guns in their hands, crowded about him; and the white men, becoming alarmed, went away.

This is the white men's version of the cause of the trouble, but the Indians tell a quite different story. One of their band, called Iowa Jim, said that the whites came upon them while they were in camp resting from their journey, gave them whisky, and made them drunk. The white men then robbed them of their horses and blankets, mistreated their women and children, and left. Recovering from their debauch, the Indians were hungry, and one of them shot a hog and brought it into camp. Big Neck rebuked the forager for this, saying, —

"It is true that wè have been robbed, and are hungry; but the hog was not ours, and you should not have shot it."

Whichever may be the true story, the settlers, after their interview with the Indians, hurried back to their cabins, and, gathering up what property they could, went with their families down into what is now Randolph County, to the home of William Blackwell, in Silver Creek settlement. In a few hours, the news of the trouble had spread throughout the little town, and a company was formed to drive the Indians out. A messenger was also dispatched to Howard County, to notify the authorities there. By ten o'clock on the morning of the 25th, a party of volunteers, numbering between forty and seventy-five men, set out for the "Cabins," under the command of Captain Trammell. They reached the place on the morning of the 27th. A council was held, and it was decided to proceed to the Indian camp, and compel the Indians to leave the country. Myers, Gross, and Cain accompanied the volunteers.

Big Neck and his band had retired some distance up the Chariton, and had gone into camp at a point near the Schuyler County line. The whites advanced to within sight of the camp, and then halted to reconnoiter. Captain Trammell swung his men around to the north, and, coming up, formed a line in the rear of the Indians. Dismounting his men, and leaving every fourth one to hold horses, the captain advanced toward the wigwams with the others, calling for the interpreter. Iowa Jim stepped forward, gun in hand, and Captain Trammell said, —

"You must leave this country at once, and stay away. The land belongs to the whites, and you have no right here."

Through his interpreter, Big Neck answered, —

"The land is ours. We will leave when we please. I am going to see the red-headed governor (General Clark) about it, and he will say I am right."

Captain Trammell was cool. He told the Indians that he did not wish to fight, but that they were trespassers in the country, and must depart. He made no serious objection to their peaceably entering the country to fish and hunt, but a permanent occupation since the recent trouble would be wholly impossible. Big Neck was inclined to assent to the demands of Trammell, and all seemed in a fair way to be adjusted without bloodshed.

But some of the whites were determined to bring on a fight. They had marched far and suffered much, and, besides, they were angry. Trammell, seeing the restless feeling of his men, rode back to the main line, which was advancing, and ordered them to keep their places. Some of the Indians were seen to take position behind trees, and hurriedly load their guns. Milton Bozarth discovered an Indian behind a tree priming his rifle. He called out to Jim Myers, whose attention was in another direction, —

"Look out, Jim, or he will shoot you!"

Jim Myers, without waiting for any orders, raised his gun and shot the Indian down. This Indian was the brother of Big Neck. As he fell, mortally wounded, he uttered a terrible yell. Powell Owenby fired, killing a little girl, the child of the Indian that Myers had just slain. William Winn shot and killed the mother of the child.

The Indian women, with characteristic shrieks and yells, began to run away, while the warriors, with guns loaded and bows strung, charged the whites. Volleys were exchanged at close quarters. The savages fought well, firing from behind trees and logs. Their steady aim, together with their war whoops and savage yells, was too much for the whites, and all but about fifteen fled at the first onset.

The main body of white men, having gained their horses, mounted and rode away; but Jim Myers, who had fired the first shot, was killed before he could reach his horse. Powell Owenby had mounted and was riding away, when the animal, maddened by the flash and report of guns, became unmanageable, and threw him into a thicket, where the Indians found him, still stunned by the fall. There they quickly shot him to death. Winn had his thigh broken by a bullet, and lay helpless on the battlefield. A number of other whites were also wounded. Captain Trammell was struck by an arrow, and rode over a hundred miles with the weapon in his body. He died a few days later from the wound.

The Indians found Winn, built a fire, and threw him upon it, but he was dragged from the flames, killed, and scalped by Big Neck. Owenby and Myers were also scalped, and then the savages left the country. An army of militia was called out, and marched to the scene of the trouble, but, as the savages had left, there was nothing for it to do but to bury the dead. Only one Indian was found, and he was some distance from the scene of the conflict, sitting against a tree, stark and stiff in death. He was richly decorated, and was supposed to be the chief's brother, whom Jim Myers had killed.

Big Neck himself and five others were afterwards arrested, tried before a jury of frontiersmen, and acquitted. This assures one that the Indians were less to blame than the whites. Big Neck never again entered Missouri. When he learned that he was to be banished from the hunting grounds of his fathers, he covered his head with his blanket, and said that he was ashamed for the sun to shine upon him.

* * * * * * * *

The Black Hawk War in Illinois in 1831–32 caused the inhabitants of north Missouri great uneasiness. Several companies and regiments were called out, and, acting on false alarms, they made some long marches but did no fighting. Blockhouses and forts were built for protection, but were not needed. However, it was no doubt due to the extraordinary precaution of the governor that an invasion of Missouri was averted. This ended the Indian troubles in Missouri.

* * * * * * * *

An important event in the history of Missouri occurred in 1837. It was the Platte purchase, by which a valuable tract of land was added to the already large State. The idea originated with General Andrew S. Hughes at a regimental muster in the summer of 1835.

At this meeting General Hughes proposed the acquisition of the Platte country, inhabited by the Sac and Fox Indians. The matter was called to the attention of Congress. Senator Benton and his colleagues in both houses were in favor of it, and an act was accordingly passed to extend the boundary of Missouri so as to include the triangle between the existing line and the Missouri River. The Indians were removed to what is now Kansas.

The Platte purchase included all that portion of the State west of a line extending from Kansas City northward to the Iowa line. As said above, this tract is now divided into the counties of Atchison, Andrew, Buchanan, Holt, Nodaway, and Platte; and to-day it is among the most fertile and beautiful portions of Missouri.

XXX.

THE MORMONS.

ABOUT the time of the expulsion of the Indians from north Missouri, the central and western portions of the State were agitated by a religious fanaticism which in some respects surpassed that of the Fanatical Pilgrims. This new religious sect called themselves the Church of Jesus Christ of Latter Day Saints; but the common name for them was Mormons. Their leader was Joseph Smith, who declared that he had received revelations from Heaven, with the command to found a new church.

He also claimed to have discovered some mysterious plates, which, by divine direction, he dug from the earth in the western part of New York State. These plates he interpreted and published as the Book of Mormon, sometimes called the Mormon Bible. He at once began preaching his new religion, and about the year 1831, with a number of converts, he removed to Kirtland, Ohio.

Historians and biographers have dealt very harshly with Joseph Smith. He is represented by some as an unprincipled, lazy fellow, who should have been sent to the penitentiary early in his career. He seems to have been subject to periodical backslidings, occasionally professing religion, then falling from grace and becoming again a drunken loafer.

At last, however, according to his own statement, the angel of the Lord appeared unto him in a vision, pardoned his sins, and told him where to find the mysterious plates upon which he was to found the church of "Latter Day Saints."

In many respects, the Mormons were like the Fanatical Pilgrims. The head of their government, spiritual and temporal, was a prophet, and, like the prophet of the pilgrims, he had visions. Like the pilgrims, also, the Mormons journeyed southwest in search of "Zion" or the New Jerusalem. It was to find this holy spot that Smith visited Missouri in 1831, and there the search ended, for Independence, Jackson County, seemed to fulfill the conditions. Smith named this place "The New Jerusalem," and then returned to Kirtland.

Next year, the prophet visited Missouri with many followers, who all located in Jackson County. They had considerable money, for they entered several hundred acres of land, most of which was west of Independence. They professed to own all things in common, which really meant, however, that the bishops and prophet owned everything. They established a newspaper, — the first in the county, — and called it *The Evening Star*. In this journal, the revelations of the prophet appeared in weekly installments. These revelations promised great things to the true believers, but foretold terrible consequences to the Gentiles, as they called all not Mormons.

The Gentiles at first merely ridiculed the prophecies thus published; but it was not long before these prophecies became bold threats. Joseph Smith and his Mormon bishops promised the faithful that they would drive out the Gentiles and take the country. They even declared their intention to unite the Indians of the north with themselves, and to drive away all opponents of Mormonism. They said that it was the Lord's country, and that the Lord's people were entitled to it.

Incensed by such expressions from press and pulpit, the Gentiles in and near Independence rose in a body, destroyed the printing office, and tarred and feathered the bishop, with one or two of his companions. This was in July, 1833. The Mormons were not slow to retaliate, and other deeds of violence led to a fray in which three men were killed. Then on November 2 the Mormons marched to destroy the town of Independence, but turned back on the appearance of a large body of Gentiles. Negotiations for peace were entered into, and it was finally decided that the Mormons were to leave that part of the country, never to return. The

Gentiles were to pay them for the *Star* printing office, and they were given until the end of the year to leave Jackson County.

The exodus commenced at once. The Mormons crossed the Missouri River and settled in Clay and Carroll counties, but afterwards moved into Caldwell County, where they built up a town called Far West. Its site is now in the middle of a cultivated field, not far from Kingston. Among its buildings was the home of Joseph Smith, — a small, substantial frame structure, of one and a half stories; and in the center of the town was left a space for a large and splendid temple. The Mormons, however, did not begin work on this temple till the year 1837, and so it was never built.

All this time the prophet and others were engaged in making converts to the new faith. Mormon missionaries spread over most of the United States and several European countries, and they sent many new believers to settle near Far West. These recruits laid out farms, built houses, and quickly changed the wilderness into a prosperous community. The Mormon settlements extended into Livingston, Carroll, Daviess, and Clinton counties. Far West was for a time their only town; but it was laid out on a grand scale, and it became an important commercial center.

Whatever else may be said of the Mormon people while in Missouri, they cannot be accused of lacking energy and industry. It is true that as a rule they were not well educated, but they were nearly always thrifty and prosperous. If their religion had been less obnoxious, and they had been more charitable to their neighbors, and if they had not adopted unlawful practices, they might have long remained a power in the State. But in addition to advocating polygamy, they still claimed that they were God's chosen children, and thus were entitled to everything.

The prosperity of the Mormon settlements drew to that part of the State many good and industrious people who did not partake of their peculiar notions. The Mormons became very jealous of these unbelievers, as they called them, and determined to drive them away. Bands of lawless Mormons began to wander over the country, plundering the Gentiles indiscriminately. Many members of the new sect were undoubtedly sincere, and desired to do right; but, beside them, under a cloak of religion and fanaticism, many bad men sought to enrich themselves.

The Gentiles, with great alarm, noticed the growing strength and proportionate lawlessness of this religious body, but were powerless to prevent them. Nearly all the offices were under Mormon control, and if a band of these robbers were arrested, they were tried before Mormon officials and juries, and were acquitted. The Gentiles had the sympathy of the people outside the Mormon districts; and, had not those misguided fanatics believed so implicitly in Joseph Smith's prophecies, they must have seen that they were laying the foundation of their own ruin. The schemes of the prophet were so wild and unreasonable as to cause one to doubt his sanity. But the followers of Black Hawk, Big Neck, and other Indian chiefs were still smarting under their defeat; and his plan to unite all the Indians with his

Mormon followers, and sweep the Gentiles from the earth, seemed not impossible to the Missourians.

A small colony of Mormons had located at De Witt, in Carroll County, and the people determined to drive them out. About this time trouble arose also between the Mormons and Gentiles in Daviess County. The people here were anxious to elect officials who would punish Mormon offenders, and the only way to do it was to disfranchise all of that sect. This was attempted at an election held near Gallatin, and a fight was the result. The citizens of Daviess County called on the people of Carroll to aid them in driving out the obnoxious foe. The men of Carroll County responded heartily; but, while they were assisting in the suppression of the disorders of their neighbors, the Mormons took advantage of their absence from home to send many recruits to De Witt.

Here the Mormons showed signs of making a stand. The Gentiles, to the number of four or five hundred, surrounded their camp, and organized a little army. Congreve Jackson, of Howard County, was elected brigadier general; Ebenezer Price, of Clay, was made colonel; Singleton Vaughn, lieutenant colonel; and Sarchel Woods, major. Under these officers, the brigade spent ten days in drilling, and then began an attack on the Mormons; but they desisted after a few shots were exchanged.

Matters were finally adjusted peaceably, when the Mormons agreed to sell their possessions to the Gentiles, and to leave the county. At the last moment, however, the arrival of Lyman Wright, a Mormon colonel, with one hundred recruits, came near inducing the Mormons to rescind their agreement to leave. But after considerable discussion, they removed to Livingston and Daviess counties.

Settlements of Mormons had grown up at a few other places, though their principal town was still Far West, and all efforts to dislodge them were, for a time, in vain. After the trouble at the election near Gallatin, the Mormons formed the plan of compelling all the Gentiles to leave the country. They resorted to every sort of violence, driving people from their homes, destroying their household goods, and burning their buildings. Mr. Levi F. Goben, a resident of Livingston County, said that he himself saw a ravine filled with the furniture of the Gentiles, which the Mormons had thrown there.

A band of destroying angels, as they called themselves, went to the house of a man named Bogard. Mr. Bogard's wife was sick, but they made her get out of bed, and leave the house, which they soon burned. She carried her babe in her arms, and, after going a little way, fell at the roadside from weakness; and then a Mormon named Allred took the ramrod from his gun and whipped her, to make her rise and travel further.

The above are only instances of the many conflicts and outrages that marked the struggle between the Mormons and their opponents. In 1838 the disorders became so serious as to threaten civil war. Mormon offenders resisted arrest, and were supported by the armed resistance of their fellow-believers. Finally, Governor Boggs issued a proclamation ordering out the militia to put down the insurrection and enforce the laws, and General Alexander W. Doniphan was sent to the scene of the trouble, with part of the first brigade of the State troops.

The Mormon force, numbering about one thousand men, was led by G. W. Hinkle. Their first encounter with the militia was a slight skirmish on Crooked River, which resulted in the killing of a Mormon named David Patton,—"Captain Fear-not," as he styled himself,— the leader of the "destroying angels."

The only engagement of any importance, however, was at Haughns Mill, about fifteen miles east of Far West. There is no official report of this battle, and the account given in this chapter is from the lips of a survivor of the bloody affray.

The election trouble in 1838, followed by the effort on the part of the Mormons to drive out the Gentiles, caused the latter to organize independent companies of rangers. This independent command at no time exceeded one hundred and fifty men. They were, for the most part, men with private grievances against the Mormons. The rangers of Daviess and Livingston counties chose as their colonel, Thomas Jennings, a soldier of 1812 who had fought under Jackson at New Orleans, and who in later years served in the Mexican War. His son, Obadiah Jennings, was made captain of one of the companies.

The entire force was composed of deer hunters and Indian fighters, who were armed with their trusty rifles. The little band, reduced by furloughs and detached parties to about eighty, was encamped at Lock Springs, to protect the Grand River settlements until the arrival of the expected militia. While the rangers were waiting there, a messenger ran into the camp, saying, —

"The Mormons at Haughns Mill are going to burn Grand River."

Jennings determined to march against Haughns Mill at once. It was not more than five miles from Lock Springs, and he reached it about three o'clock in the afternoon. The mill was situated on Shoal Creek, and there was a blacksmith's shop west of it and about fifty yards away. A dam had been thrown across the creek to force the water into the mill race. Two or three log cabins were built on the west side of the stream, and one or two on the east side. A well had just been dug close to the blacksmith's shop, and on this afternoon the Mormons, to the number of forty or fifty, were assembled about it.

When Jennings came in sight of the mill, his men struck up a martial air with the fife and drum. The Mormons seized their guns, and all that could, crowded into the shop. Some got behind it, and a few started across the creek on the dam.

The Gentiles opened fire, and pressed forward upon the enemy. There was no time for parley, and both sides were determined neither to give nor to ask quarter.

Mounted on his white horse, Colonel Jennings rode up and down the line, encouraging his men by word and act. The old deer hunters sent their bullets with fatal effect through the chinks between the logs into the blacksmith's shop. The Mormons returned the fire, but every time their heads appeared at the cracks, they were struck by bullets. So they kept their heads down, and, poking their guns through the cracks, fired without taking aim. In this manner they shot over the heads of the Gentiles.

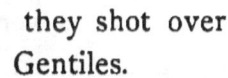

Ira Glaze and Jesse Nave, both experienced deer hunters, ran up to the side of the shop, and poked their guns through the chinks until the muzzles almost touched the men inside. The Mormons tried to shoot these bold rangers, but they hugged the outside walls close, and kept out of range. Occasionally Glaze was heard to shout, —

"Your powder burnt me that time."

During the remainder of the fight, these two daring men remained just on the outside of the shop, loading and firing through the cracks at the men within.

One Mormon leaped from the shop, and, running to the creek, fled across on the mill dam, and reached a field beyond. He might have escaped, had he not climbed on a fence and paused to look back. Frank Berry, an old deer hunter, saw him, leveled his unerring rifle, and fired. The Mormon dropped his gun, threw up his hands, and fell from the fence into the field.

Another Mormon escaped from the blacksmith's shop, and was running up Shoal Creek, when a Gentile named Jake Rodgers saw him and gave chase. Jake's rifle was empty, and he had no other weapon but a sword made out of a scythe. The Mormon, seeing that he could not outrun the fleet Gentile, dropped his gun; then, turning, he threw up his hands, and begged for his life. But he appealed in vain. Rodgers ran upon him, cut him down, and hacked him to death.

No prisoners were taken; for all who did not escape were slain. Even a boy who had crawled under the bellows in the shop perished with the others. The firing from the outside continued until no response came from the shop. Then, pushing open the door, the rangers found the dark room tenanted only by the dead. The exact number of Mormons killed is not known. History puts the number at eighteen or twenty; but an eyewitness who helped collect the dead said that he counted thirty-three.

The dead Mormons were thrown into the newly dug well, and were covered up. The men under Colonel Jennings soon afterwards joined the forces under Doniphan, and all marched to capture Far West. Here the Mormons had fortified themselves for an attack; but, at last realizing the folly of resistance, they agreed to dispose of their possessions and leave the State. Their property was sold at a great sacrifice, and they left Missouri, never to return. Joseph Smith and some of the other leaders were arrested, but made their escape; and others, who were put on trial, were acquitted by juries.

In 1841, an attempt was made to assassinate Governor Boggs, — as was supposed, by a Mormon named Porter Rockwell, — but the attempt was a failure. The Mormons went to Illinois, where they again had trouble with the Gentiles. Joseph Smith and his brother Hyrum were killed, and the others were driven from the State. They went to Utah, and under new leaders established another home in the wilderness — Salt Lake City, which is their capital to-day

XXXI.

THE HONEY WAR.—COLONEL GENTRY.

GOVERNOR LYMAN BOGGS, under whose administration the Mormons were expelled from the State, found his entire term filled with foreign and domestic trouble. In 1839, the year after the Mormons were expelled, the whole State was thrown into a fever of excitement by a conflict which threatened war in north Missouri.

The trouble arose over the disputed boundary line between Missouri and Iowa. The tract of land in question was mostly forest; and, as it was noted for wild bees, the dispute was ironically called the "Honey War."

Instead of pursuing a sensible policy and having the boundary line settled according to law, Missouri and Iowa both stubbornly insisted on levying taxes and executing writs in the disputed territory. A man living in this region could not tell where he belonged.

A Missouri sheriff, while trying to execute papers here, was driven away by the Iowa officers. Governor Boggs of Missouri called out the militia to enforce the writs of the State. Governor Lucas of Iowa ordered out the Iowa militia to uphold the laws of his Territory. For several weeks, two armies of two or three thousand men each were confronting each other, and a bloody conflict was hourly expected.

The affair took a ridiculous turn, however, and became a huge joke; bloodshed was averted, and anger changed to mirth. Mr. Campbell, of Palmyra, wrote some doggerel verse which burlesqued the two governors and set everybody to thinking what a ludicrous figure they were cutting. The first two stanzas of Mr. Campbell's poetic effusion were as follows:—

THE HONEY WAR.

Ye freemen of this happy land,
  Which flows with milk and honey,
Arise! To arms! Your ponies mount!
  Regard not blood or money.
Old Governor Lucas, tigerlike,
  Is prowling round our borders,
But Governor Boggs is wide awake—
  Just listen to his orders.

"Three bee trees stand about the line
  Between our State and Lucas.
Be ready all these trees to fall
  And bring things to a focus.
We'll show old Lucas how to brag,
  And seize our precious honey!
He also claims, I understand,
  Of us three bits in money."

Seeing the folly of going to war over the disputed boundary, the Clark County (Mo.) court appointed a committee to wait on the Iowa Territorial Legislature, then in session at Burlington, and try to bring about an amicable settlement of the difficulties. The committee was kindly received, and resolutions were adopted asking the governors of Missouri and Iowa to suspend hostilities until the boundary line could be determined by the national government.

Congress established this line in 1840. The decision was in favor of Iowa, and "the Indian boundary line" run by Colonel Sullivan was declared to be the true northern boundary of Missouri. The decision was accepted by all. A few years later, the line was run by commissioners from Iowa and Missouri, and some corrections were made in the former survey. Their determination of the boundary fixed the line as it exists to-day.

* * * * * * * *

When the Seminole Indians in Florida had proved too much for the regular army of the United States, the President asked Senator Benton if some of the Missourians would go there to fight them. Mr. Benton answered that the Missourians would go wherever their services were needed. A requisition was accordingly made on Governor Boggs for two regiments of mounted volunteers.

The first regiment enlisted for the service in Florida was commanded by Colonel Richard Gentry. The men assembled at Columbia early in October, 1837, and marched to Jefferson Barracks, near St. Louis, where they were formally mustered into service by the general in command. Then they floated down the Mississippi River in boats to New Orleans, where some sailing vessels were employed to carry them to Florida.

They were overtaken by a violent storm on the voyage, and several of their vessels were stranded. Some horses were lost, but no soldiers. On November 15 the regiment landed at Tampa Bay, Florida, and went into camp to await orders from Colonel Taylor, who was then in command of the United States troops. They remained here for fifteen days; and on December 1 they received orders from Taylor to join the regular troops and advance to Okechobee Lake, which was over one hundred miles distant. It was reported that the Seminoles had gathered there, and were prepared for battle, under their most successful leaders, Sam Jones, Tiger Tail, Alligator, and Mycanopee.

The march inland was uneventful until the little army came to the Kissimmee River. Here a few Indians who were guarding their cattle were captured, and from them it was learned that the hostile force was close by. On December 25, having crossed the river, the white men advanced to give battle. Colonel Taylor placed the Missouri volunteers in the center and in front, with the regular troops supporting the flanks.

The Indians had carefully posted themselves on the edge of a swamp. Their ground was well chosen, and they fought more stubbornly than the savages usually did.

Colonel Gentry's command, owing to the nature of the ground, dismounted and fought on foot. The colonel himself was on foot also. After several hours' severe fighting, the Indians began to fall back, and Colonel Gentry ordered his men to advance. The Indians were being slowly driven from the field, when the Missouri colonel was fatally wounded in the abdomen.

Though he suffered the most intense pain, and knew that his wound was mortal, yet he remained on his feet for an hour after he was shot, and led his men on to victory. At last human endurance could hold out no longer, and he sank to the earth at the head of his regiment. He was carried from the field and died that night.

The fall of their gallant colonel did not dishearten the Missourians. They kept on fighting until the Indians were put to flight, and Colonel Taylor ordered them to take care of the fallen. The killed and wounded among the whites numbered one hundred and thirty-eight, most of whom were Missourians.

The services of the Missouri volunteers being no longer required, they returned to their homes in 1838, and were mustered out of service. The body of Colonel Gentry, with those of Captain Van Swearingen and Lieutenants Brooke and Center, of the regular army, were brought to Jefferson Barracks to be buried.

Gentry County, organized February 12, 1841, was named in honor of this dauntless Missouri colonel.

In his official report of the battle of Okechobee, Colonel Taylor did great injustice to the Missouri volunteers. He represented them as breaking ranks and flying to the rear of the army, and said that all efforts to rally them were in vain. Taylor, like all regular army officers, was inclined to hold the volunteers in contempt, notwithstanding the fact that in actual war they do nine tenths of the fighting. Though Colonel Gentry had fallen in the front, fighting the enemy, and though his men, with a very few exceptions, remained on the field until victory was gained, the report of the commander branded them all as cowards.

So manifestly unjust and untruthful was Taylor's report, that the Missouri Legislature resented it, and ordered an investigation into the conduct of the Missourians engaged in the Florida war.

A number of officers appeared before the investigating committee. Their sworn statements were in conflict with the report of Colonel Taylor, and the Legislature passed strong resolutions condemning this report, and asking the federal government to order an investigation into the conduct of the Missouri volunteers. Though the resolutions passed both houses without a dissenting voice, they were never acted upon by the President of the United States.

Colonel Richard Gentry.

XXXII.

DONIPHAN AND PRICE.

Colonel Alexander W. Doniphan.

WHEN a quarrel arose between Mexico and the United States, which resulted in a war, the Missourians did not stop to inquire as to which was the just side in the difficulty. Their country wanted soldiers, and they were quick to respond to the demand.

It was on May 13, 1846, that Congress made a formal declaration of war with Mexico. Immediately afterwards, Governor Edwards of Missouri issued a call for volunteers to join the "Army of the West," which was under the command of General Stephen Kearney, and was soon to begin the conquest of northern Mexico by marching against Santa Fé. Mounted volunteers were quickly enlisted in Missouri, and were collected at Fort Leavenworth, the point where the army was to begin its march. On June 18, all the companies of the first regiment had arrived there, and an election was held, which resulted in the choice of Alexander W. Doniphan as colonel; C. F. Ruff, lieutenant colonel; and William Gilpin, major.

Colonel Doniphan's command was the very flower of Missouri riflemen. They were armed with what was known as the United States Yager, an improvement on the musket, and a very accurate weapon; and each man was a sharpshooter. Only a part, however, of the Missouri volunteers were cavalry. There was a battalion of light artillery from St. Louis under the command of Captain R. A. Weightman and Captain A. W. Fischer, and two battalions of infantry from Platte and Cole counties, commanded by Captain Murphy and Captain Augney. The "Laclede Rangers," from St. Louis, were under Captain Thomas B. Hudson. Including the regular United States troops, the expedition was made up of one thousand six hundred and fifty-eight men; and it was provided with sixteen pieces of ordnance — twelve six pounders, and four twelve-pound howitzers.

The march of Kearney and Doniphan extended across what is now Kansas, a part of the Indian Territory, and New Mexico; and it was perhaps the boldest invasion, by so small a body of men, ever made into the heart of an enemy's country. They were practically cut off from all supplies and communications; and the hardships and sufferings of their men are almost beyond belief. One of the soldiers in describing the journey said: —

"We traveled for days with very little water, and what we did find was so brackish we could not use it.

The sand rolled up in clouds about us, and settled on our clothing, hands, and faces, until the color of the soldiers could not be told by looking at them. I have raked the dry sand off my tongue with my finger. One day we came to a bright, clear stream of water, but it was almost scalding hot.

"When night came, worn out, and parched with thirst, we were compelled to sleep on the ground, our blanket furnishing our only bed and covering. The plains seemed to swarm with lizards. A soldier would scarcely get to sleep when the active little reptiles began crawling over him. They glided over our faces, and crawled up our trousers, and sometimes a soldier's blanket would become so full of them that he would get up and shake them off upon a sleeping companion. A sleeping soldier was often heard to say, —

"'Don't shake your lizards on me!'

"But perhaps he was too drowsy to resent it. In a few moments he would be awakened by the active, creeping reptiles, and arising would shake them on some other sleeping comrade."

From Fort Leavenworth to Santa Fé, the march was through a wilderness or uninhabited desert; but the soldiers bore up bravely, and made little or no complaint. After the capture of Santa Fé, the little army was divided; Kearney went on to conquer California, while Doniphan advanced toward central Mexico. On December 25, Doniphan's regiment reached the Brazito, or "Little Arm" River, where they had their first encounter with the Mexicans.

It is said that the colonel and some of his officers

were playing cards in the camp, when they discovered a cloud of dust approaching them. It proved to be Captain Reid's scouts, who came to tell them that a large body of the enemy was advancing to attack them. Colonel Doniphan threw down his cards, and drew his sword, saying, —

"Boys, I held an invincible hand, but we shall have to play it out in steel now."

Every man flew to his post. The bugle sounded, and the long roll of the drum announced the proximity of the enemy. The men threw down the loads of wood and buckets of water which they were carrying to their camp, and, seizing their rifles, fell into line of battle. A large body of Mexicans was seen on the level plain bordering the Brazito.

The Missouri troops, amounting to about eight hundred in number, were commanded by Colonel Doniphan in person. The Mexicans, about eleven hundred strong, were under General Ponce de Leon, an officer of considerable experience. His men were all veterans, and the force was not to be despised.

While the two armies stood confronting each other in line of battle, General Ponce de Leon dispatched a lieutenant to Colonel Doniphan, bearing a black flag. The messenger rode at full speed until within sixty yards of the American lines, when he halted and saluted with his ensign. Colonel Doniphan, with his interpreter, T. Caldwell, advanced toward him, and asked what he wanted. The messenger said, —

"The Mexican general summons your commander to appear before him."

"If your general desires peace, let him come here," was the interpreter's answer.

"Does your commander refuse to come? Then we will break your ranks, and take him there."

"Come and take him."

The Mexican flew into a rage, and cried,—

"Prepare for a charge,—we neither ask nor give quarter." Waving his black flag over his head, he galloped back to the Mexican lines.

As soon as he had reached his friends, there came a trumpet blast, and a body of Mexican dragoons was seen to gallop boldly forward. Colonel Doniphan cried,—

"Steady, boys! Don't be too eager to fire. Wait until they are near enough to make it count. We have not brought our powder and bullets across the plains to throw them away. Remember you are Missourians."

His men began to cheer, and when the Mexicans were within a few rods, opened fire on them. Several saddles were emptied, and the enemy was thrown into confusion. Then Captain Reid, with sixteen cavalrymen, charged through their line and drove them back.

A body of Mexican infantry came up behind a thicket and opened fire on the riflemen. Colonel Doniphan shouted, —

"Lie down on your faces, and reserve your fire until the Mexicans come within sixty paces."

After the Mexicans had fired three volleys, they saw the Americans lying on the ground, and supposed that they had slain all the invaders. They rushed forward, shouting, —

"Bueno! Bueno!" (Good! Good!)

Suddenly a volley of rifle balls mowed down a large number of them, and those uninjured retreated in confusion. The battle was stubborn, but the Missouri riflemen and artillerists were too much for the Mexicans. General Ponce de Leon and sixty of his men were killed, five were made prisoners, one hundred and fifty were wounded, and the remainder fled.

Doniphan had eight wounded, but none killed. Soon after this battle he advanced and took possession of El Paso.

The principal conflict in which the Missourians under Doniphan were engaged was in the Sacramento Pass, near the city of Chihuahua, February 28, 1847. At this pass, the Mexicans numbered between four and five thousand, under Major-General José A. Heredia. Colonel Doniphan had but nine hundred and twenty-four men, and ten pieces of artillery.

One of Doniphan's officers, when he saw how well the Mexicans were posted, and how greatly superior their numbers were, went to the colonel and said,—

"Colonel, there are great odds against us."

"About six to one."

"And they are strongly intrenched!"

"They certainly could not have a stronger position."

"Then how do you hope to win?"

Doniphan gave him a look of surprise, and said, —

"*Why, we are Missourians.*"

The officer saluted, and was silent. The battle lasted three hours, but the Missouri riflemen stormed redoubt after redoubt, and sent the enemy flying in every direction.

Just before the charge, the right and left wings were ordered to dismount, and every seventh man was detailed to hold horses. Volleys of musketry, grape, and canister from the enemy's works maddened the men who were kept out of the fray by this unwelcome duty. As Colonel Doniphan was passing up the lines, a volunteer who had seven horses in charge called to him and said,—

"See here, Colonel! Am I compelled to stand here in this tempest of cannon and musket balls, and hold horses?"

"Yes, if you were detailed for that purpose."

The volunteer, eager to have a hand in the fight, tied the several bridles together, threw them down, seized his gun and saber, and started off in the charge, saying, —

"Hold horses, nothing! I didn't come here to hold horses; I can do that at home."

While this showed a lack of discipline appalling to a regular army officer, it also showed an enthusiasm which explains Doniphan's wonderful victory.

As the right wing scaled the breastworks, Sergeant Tom Hinckle was among the first to cross the intrenchments. He was in advance of the others, and soon found himself surrounded by the enraged enemy. Firing his Yager and pistols, and not having time to reload them, he seized stones and hurled them with such fearful rapidity and effect as to force the Mexicans back, and thus held the ground until the others came to aid him in driving the enemy from the field.

Major Samuel C. Owens, of Independence, Missouri, was the only American killed. There were eleven wounded, of whom three died of their wounds. The Mexican loss was three hundred and four killed, forty prisoners, and nearly five hundred wounded.

Next day, Colonel Doniphan took possession of the city of Chihuahua, which was the chief object of the long march. His little band of brave soldiers returned by way of the Gulf of Mexico and the Mississippi River to Missouri, where they were mustered out of service.

* * * * * * * *

Another noted leader of Missouri troops in the Mexican War was Sterling Price. When the war broke out he was a member of Congress, but he soon resigned his seat in order to organize a second regiment of volunteers in his State. One full regiment and two battalions were enlisted,— all but one battalion being mounted.

After coming together at Fort Leavenworth, the men elected Price as their colonel, and D. D. Mitchell, lieutenant colonel. Price's instructions were to reinforce the Army of the West, and he led his force to Santa Fé by the same route that Kearney and Doniphan had taken.

While in command of the American troops in New Mexico, Price was called upon to put down a formidable revolt against the United States. His first encounter with the insurgent Mexicans was at Canada, January 24, 1847. The Americans were victorious, and, pushing on, soon put the enemy to flight in a second battle, though outnumbered. Then the Mexicans and their Indian allies sought refuge in Taos, which was strongly fortified. Colonel Price arrived at the town on February 3, and the next morning advanced to take it. The enemy offered a stubborn resistance, and the fight lasted all day. When the Mexicans finally surrendered, they had lost over two hundred and fifty men killed, while the American loss was but fifteen killed and fifty wounded.

This was the last battle fought by Colonel Price in the Mexican War, as the people of New Mexico soon submitted. The final treaty of peace with Mexico gave to the United States a vast amount of territory, in which was included most of the region that had been conquered by the Missouri volunteers.

XXXIII.

BORDER TROUBLE.

FROM the time that Missouri was admitted as a State, down to the Civil War, there was almost constant agitation over slavery. The strife extended throughout the whole nation, but in Missouri it was especially bitter, for the people were very evenly divided on the subject.

In 1828 there was a strong disposition on the part of Missouri statesmen to abolish slavery. The two United States senators, Benton and Barton, with the members of Congress from Missouri, met with a number of prominent State politicians in St. Louis, to devise some scheme for liberating the slaves.

The plan agreed upon was that of gradual emancipation. It provided that after a certain time every slave born in the State should be free at the age of twenty-one, and that the master should be compelled to teach him to read and write.

Before the Missouri leaders were ready to submit the plan to the people, however, an abolitionist in New York, named Arthur Tappan, invited two negro men to dine at his house with him. In the afternoon of the same day, these negroes were seen riding in a carriage with Tappan's daughters about the streets of the city.

This incident was published in all the papers, and so aroused public sentiment against the abolitionists, that Benton and his friends dared not submit their proposition to the people.

It may seem strange at this day that the silly act of a New York fanatic should change the mind of the people of Missouri. But people in the slaveholding States believed that if the negroes were freed they would be placed on a social equality with the whites. The thought was repugnant, and the conduct of Tappan seemed to prove that social equality was what the abolitionists desired.

For some time after the Tappan episode, there was a lull in the slavery agitation, but in 1833, Elijah P. Lovejoy, a graduate from Princeton, came to St. Louis and began the publication of an abolition paper. He was a reformer whose intentions, doubtless, were good; but his lectures and editorials were unfavorably received.

There were many things at that time which were prejudicial to the success of Lovejoy. Tappan's foolish act was not forgotten. Then, too, the abolitionists were assisting many negroes to escape from the State by a system of "underground railroads," as they were called. Some of these runaway negroes were vicious fellows, and before escaping from their masters, committed the most horrible crimes.

One negro woman poisoned her master and his whole family. A runaway negro man in Marion County murdered a little girl and boy whom he found playing in the woods. A second negro woman, left in charge of three small children, in a fit of frenzy struck one over the head with a board, and killed it. She then seized a hatchet, killed the other two to prevent them from reporting her crime, and fled to the woods. The abolitionists, by means of their underground railroad system, enabled her to elude all pursuit and escape to Canada, and she was never brought to justice for her terrible crime.

The horrible outrages of the runaway negroes were attributed by some to the influence of the abolitionists. The charge was no doubt unjust, but there were many people in the Southern States who believed that the abolitionists were inciting the slaves not only to run away, but to murder their masters as well.

Wild rumors were often heard of some plot on the part of the slaves to rise and kill their masters while asleep. Although the rumors were in time found to be groundless, they tended to increase the bitter feeling which the slaveholders entertained against the abolitionists.

Lovejoy found it uphill work to convert the Missourians to his ideas of emancipation. Mr. Hamilton R. Gamble, his friend, advised him "to distrust his own judgment so far as to pass over in silence everything connected with slavery."

"I will not," he answered. "I have sworn eternal enmity to slavery, and, being determined, by the blessing of God I will never go back."

The proslavery people became so incensed against him, that he left St. Louis and located at Alton, in Illinois. Here he was attacked by a mob. He fired

into it, killing one man, and then was himself killed by the others.

During this time there lived in St. Louis Dr. Emerson, a surgeon in the United States army, who owned a young negro named Dred Scott. When Dr. Emerson was ordered to Rock Island, Illinois, in 1834, he took the negro with him. There, Scott met a female slave belonging to Major Taliaferro, of the army, and, with the consent of their masters, these two slaves were married. They were taken to Fort Snelling (in what is now Minnesota), where they lived for four or five years. Then Dr. Emerson purchased Scott's wife and two children, and took the whole family to St. Louis.

Dred Scott sued for his freedom on the plea of involuntary residence in a free State and Territory for several years; and the local court at St. Louis decided in his favor. The Supreme Court of the State, however, reversed the decision, and the case was finally taken to the Supreme Court of the United States, where Chief-Justice Roger B. Taney delivered the famous "Dred Scott decision" in 1857.

In that decision, the judge declared that the framers and supporters of the Declaration of Independence did not include the negro race in their proclamation that "all men are created equal." He said the negroes "had for more than a century before been regarded as beings of an inferior order, and altogether unfit to associate with the white race, either in social or political relations, and so far inferior that they had no rights which the white man was bound to respect, and that the negro might justly and lawfully be reduced to slavery for his benefit." Judge Taney went further in this famous decision, and declared the Missouri Compromise Act unconstitutional, null, and void.

This decision alarmed the abolitionists, for it opened up all the country once more to the spread of slavery, especially the new Territories and States yet to be formed. Moreover, the discussion of the slavery question had revived an old theory of the national union, advocated first by Aaron Burr, and afterward by John C. Calhoun, a prominent Southern statesman.

This was known as the States' sovereignty doctrine. Many men argued that each State was sovereign in itself, that the United States was only a union or compact of so many sovereign States for their mutual benefit; and that each State had a right to withdraw from the confederation or union at any time it felt disposed to do so, and set up an independent government.

The people who held this doctrine were known as States'-rights men, and their opponents were called Unionists. Those in favor of "States' rights" were, for the most part, Southerners and proslavery men, while the people in the Northern and Middle States were Unionists. The theory of States' rights was the fundamental cause of the great Civil War.

For a long time before the Dred Scott decision, the slavery question had been kept constantly before the people of Missouri. Early in 1849, Mr. Claiborne F. Jackson, a member of the State Senate, introduced a resolution in that body, denying the right of Congress to meddle with slavery in a State or Territory. His resolution absolved the slave States from the Missouri Compromise, and indirectly prepared the way for the spread of slavery in the new States and Territories.

Senator Benton strongly opposed this resolution; and, when it passed the Legislature, he appealed to the people. This act is called in history "Benton's appeal." It caused his defeat when he came up for reëlection to the United States Senate in 1851, and retired him from office forever, excepting one term in the lower house of Congress. In 1856, he was a candidate for Governor of Missouri, but was defeated by Trusten Polk. He died in Washington, D.C., April 10, 1858.

In 1854 the Territories of Kansas and Nebraska were formed. Kansas was becoming well populated, and it was known that it would soon apply for admission as a State. According to the Missouri Compromise, it should be admitted as a free State; but the act creating the Territory ignored this compromise (which was later declared unconstitutional), and provided that Kansas should decide for itself whether or not it would admit slavery within its borders.

The free-State men and the proslavery men made great efforts to fill up the Territory with those of their own way of thinking before the time came for voting on the question; and the conflicts between them along the border of Missouri sometimes resulted in bloodshed. One might think that this State would have minded her own business, and not have meddled with affairs across the line; but the people of Missouri seemed to think that they ought to be consulted in regard to the political beliefs of their neighbor. Some Missourians became so interested in the kind of a constitution that Kansas should adopt, that they went over into that Territory and voted at the constitutional election. The people of Kansas, especially those of free-soil notions, objected to this neighborly assistance, and the struggle between the two parties soon broke out in civil war.

John Brown, a noted abolitionist, went to Kansas with his sons, and organized a band of armed men, who were determined that Kansas should come in as a free State. At Osawatomie, in Kansas, they had a battle with a party of proslavery men, in which several were killed and wounded. Brown and his sons were accused of murdering an old man and his family, and were compelled to fly from the Territory.

Brown last appeared in Virginia in 1859, where he tried to induce the slaves to rise against their masters. With two of his sons, some negroes, and a few white men, he seized the United States arsenal at Harpers Ferry. Here he was besieged, his sons were killed, and he and his party were captured. He was indicted for treason, and was hanged December 2, 1859.

While civil war raged in Kansas, there was much trouble also on the Missouri border. This afforded an excuse for horse thieves and outlaws to commit depredations which disgrace civilization. The outlaws of the free-soil men were called jayhawkers; those of the pro-slavery men, guerrillas and border ruffians. The outrages committed along the Missouri border, from 1856 to the close of the Civil War, are beyond description. Houses were burned, stock driven away, and people robbed and murdered. Every person who had a grudge against another took advantage of the distracted times to satisfy it.

Mr. Watson, a quiet, inoffensive man living near the Kansas line, had retired to bed one night. A voice called at his gate, —

"Hello!"

He rose, partly dressed himself, and with a lighted candle in his hand went to the door.

"What do you want?" he asked.

"We want your scalp!" shouted a voice from the road. Then followed two or three shots, and he fell dead in his doorway. His wife ran to him, and the assassins galloped away. It was never known why Mr. Watson was killed.

A party of men called at a house in the same neighborhood one dark night, and asked for the head of the family. They were told that he was absent.

"No, he isn't; tell him to come out here!" roared a voice from the darkness.

"I assure you he is not at home," stammered the frightened wife.

"Then come out yourself."

The woman and her daughter went toward the horsemen, and were seized and bound. When sure that there were no men in the house, the outlaws entered, robbed it of all valuables they could carry with them, and then, releasing their prisoners, galloped away.

In 1856, horse stealing and robbery were of almost nightly occurrence, and murder was quite frequent.

Bands of robbers on both sides increased by their outrages the difficulties between the free-State and pro-slavery men. The Governor of Missouri visited the scene of trouble, then hurried home expecting a dispatch from the President ordering out the militia of the State. Civil war was already raging along the border.

At Lexington, five hundred men were under arms. Jackson, Clay, and Platte counties were each to furnish the same number. In all, three thousand men from Missouri awaited the order of the governor to march to the scene of trouble.

But the order never came, though a guerrilla warfare continued along the border, until it was swallowed up in the great Civil War.

XXXIV.

A SEASON OF DOUBT.

THE year 1856 showed a large increase in the new political party, called the Republican. This party was known to favor limiting the territory of slavery, if not abolishing it entirely. In 1860, the Republicans nominated Abraham Lincoln for President. The Democratic party became divided in its convention, one wing nominating Stephen A. Douglas, and the other J. C. Breckenridge. The party calling itself "the Constitutional Union party" nominated John Bell. Lincoln, the Republican candidate, was elected.

The proslavery people were filled with dismay and indignation. They believed that the threat of so many years was about to be fulfilled, but still many wise men in the South advocated a peace policy.

"Give Lincoln a trial," they said; but others declared it was of no use.

"He was elected to free the negroes, and by some hook or crook he will accomplish it." Excitement was great. South Carolina seceded, other Southern States followed, and it was easily seen that most, if not all, of the slave States would soon do likewise.

Claiborne F. Jackson, of Howard County, had been elected as a Democrat to succeed Governor Robert M.

Stewart, and early in January, 1861, he was inaugurated Governor of Missouri. The great question which then agitated the minds of the people was, "Shall the State secede, or remain in the Union?" Governor Stewart's farewell message ended with a thrilling appeal for the maintenance of the Union, but it was known that his successor's views were somewhat different.

In his inaugural message Governor Jackson argued that the destiny of all the slaveholding States in the Union was the same; that it would be impossible to separate Missouri's fate from that of her sister States who had the same social organization; and that if the existing Union should be disrupted, interest and sympathy would combine to unite the fortunes of all slaveholding States. He declared that Missouri would not shrink from the duty which her position upon the border imposed, but would "stand by the South." The State, he said, was in favor of remaining in the Union so long as there was any hope of maintaining the guarantees of the Constitution; but he opposed the plan of coercing the seceded States back into the Union.

Holding the above views concerning the interests and policy of the State, the governor believed that it was Missouri's right and duty to take part in the settlement of the questions then at issue. Hence he asked the Legislature to issue an immediate call for a State convention, in order "that the will of the people may be ascertained and effectuated." He also declared that it might soon become necessary to send delegates to a convention of the Southern States, or of all the States.

The message of Governor Jackson caused widespread

alarm among all who had determined to remain loyal to the Union. It was an expression of secession in language as bold as he dared utter.

The Legislature proceeded at once to pass a bill for calling a State convention. During the discussion of the measure, the line between the Unionists and secessionists was clearly drawn. Mr. Randolph proposed to amend the original bill so that the State could not secede without the question being first submitted by vote to the people. This measure was opposed by the men who were determined to force the State out of the Union.

Mr. Lacy, from Cape Girardeau, offered a substitute for Mr. Randolph's amendment. This provided that the convention, when assembled, should have no power to change the existing relations of the State of Missouri to the government of the United States, or of any State thereof, until the act, ordinance, or resolution making such change was submitted to the people of Missouri, and approved by a majority of the qualified voters voting at the election.

The extreme secessionists opposed this substitute as strongly as they did the original amendment. But it was carried in the House, and, after some slight amendments in the Senate, it passed both houses. This was a great victory for the Union men. They had confidence in the people of Missouri, and believed that if the question of secession were submitted to them, they would vote it down.

Hon. Daniel R. Russel, a commissioner from Mississippi, was in Jefferson City at this time. His mission was to express an earnest hope that Missouri would coöperate with the South in the adoption of measures for the common defense and safety of the slaveholding States. But the bill which had just passed both branches of the Legislature made it apparent that Missouri did not intend to act hastily in the matter.

This was in January, 1861, before the inauguration of President Lincoln. The whole State, and in fact the whole nation, was in doubt and suspense. Wildest rumors flew everywhere. Governor Jackson claimed to be a Union man, but always with the proviso that the national government should not interfere with the seceded States.

To adjust matters amicably, and avoid a threatened civil war, the Peace Congress, as it was called, was proposed. It was held in Washington, D.C., February 4, 1861, and the people of Missouri took great interest in its efforts. It was hoped that the Peace Congress would agree upon some satisfactory and honorable plan of reconciling the interests of the North and the South, and of averting the danger of civil war. Waldo P. Johnson, John D. Coulter, A. W. Doniphan, Harrison Hough, and A. H. Buckner were sent to Washington as commissioners from Missouri to this Congress. Ex-President John Tyler, of Virginia, was chosen as its presiding officer. It failed to accomplish what had been hoped for, however, and its proceedings do not concern Missouri.

Waldo P. Johnson was elected to the United States Senate from Missouri in March, 1861, but had not served a year when both he and Trusten Polk, the other senator from Missouri, were expelled from that body for sympathy and participation in the war against the Union.

Meanwhile, all eyes were upon the governor and Legislature. Notwithstanding the passage of the bill calling for a convention, there were many who feared that before Lincoln's inauguration the extreme secessionists would force the State out of the Union.

On February 18, 1861, delegates to the State convention were elected. There was an active, and in some places an exciting, canvass. According to the law, each senatorial district was entitled to three times as many delegates as it had members in the Senate. The question of secession, so far as the people were concerned, was practically settled by that election; for a majority of eighty thousand votes was cast against it.

The convention assembled in the courthouse at Jefferson City, February 28, 1861, just four days before the inauguration of President Lincoln. Hon. Hamilton R. Gamble, a pronounced Unionist, was the soul and spirit of that assembly. He swayed it at will, so much so that it was called the "Gamble convention."

Perhaps a wiser choice of delegates to a convention was never made. Some of the greatest statesmen and lawyers in Missouri composed it. They steered the Ship of State through the early storm of war, and kept her off the rock of secession on which so many of her Southern sisters were wrecked.

XXXV.

CAMP JACKSON.

THE expressions in Governor Jackson's inaugural message were sufficient to arouse the apprehensions of all lovers of the Union. These apprehensions were soon afterwards greatly increased by the governor's calling out the State Guard, under General D. M. Frost.

At this time there were in the St. Louis arsenal forty thousand muskets and bayonets, and other munitions of war. When General Frost, though declaring the best intentions, began to assemble the State Guard near the arsenal, it was believed to be his design to seize the arms, and equip these militiamen as a part of the Southern army.

Major William H. Bell was commander of the arsenal. He was evidently in sympathy with the Southern cause, for he even expressed a willingness to turn over the arms to the guards. But this was early in January, and so confident were the secessionists that Missouri would be "voted out of the Union" on the 18th of February, that they were unwilling to precipitate matters. The correspondence between Governor Jackson and D. M. Frost shows treasonable intent toward the government.

There was a loyal, watchful man in St. Louis, named

Francis P. Blair, who determined to save the State for the Union. In connection with O. D. Filley, he began quietly to organize and discipline a regiment for the purpose of preventing the arsenal at St. Louis from falling into the hands of the secessionists. This was necessary, for the arsenal was guarded by not more than forty men, under a commander whose loyalty one may doubt. A Union safety committee, appointed by the President and Secretary of War, was organized in January, 1861. It was composed of the following distinguished citizens of St. Louis: O. D. Filley, chairman, James O. Broadhead, secretary, General Francis P. Blair, John How, Samuel T. Glover, and J. J. Witzig. Companies were organized and secretly drilled in O. D. Filley's store for mutual protection in case of a secessionist attack. 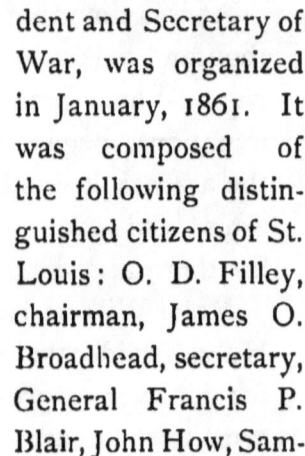 By the foresight and watchfulness of Filley and Blair, an army was quietly prepared for Captain Lyon, when no one dreamed that there was more than a handful of soldiers to defend the cause of the Union.

On the 11th of January, there arrived some reinforcements of regular soldiers at the barracks, and on the 24th of the same month, while Frost was congratulating Governor Jackson on the ease with which they could arm the soldiers, Major Bell was relieved and Major Hagner took his place. This disconcerted the plans of Frost and Jackson; and when on February 18, the day for the election of delegates to the State convention, the people declared so emphatically against secession, any one less blinded than Jackson would have seen the folly and ruin of continuing his course.

On February 6, Captain Nathaniel Lyon of the regular army arrived at the arsenal in St. Louis. He is described as "a small, angular man, with abundant sandy hair, and a coarse, reddish-brown beard. He had deep-set blue eyes, features rough and homely, and the weather-beaten aspect of a man who had seen much service on the frontier."

General Harney was in command of the Department of Missouri, and came to St. Louis about the time of the arrival of Captain Lyon. The commander, however, had many friends and relatives in sympathy with the South, and, soon after the inauguration of President Lincoln, he was ordered to Washington to explain his own views.

His departure left Lyon in command, and the captain determined to seize the opportunity to act. The State Guard under General D. M. Frost was encamped just without the city, at a place named Camp Jackson in honor of the governor of the State.

Captain Lyon was justified in his suspicions of the commander of the State Guard, for Frost was acting under Jackson, who was an avowed secessionist. After the fall of Fort Sumter, President Lincoln made his first call for seventy-five thousand men. Missouri's quota was fixed at four regiments, which Governor Jackson was requested to furnish. In reply to the demand, the governor, on April 17, 1861, defiantly informed Hon. Simon Cameron, Secretary of War, that he regarded the requisition as illegal, unconstitutional, and revolutionary; that its object was inhuman and diabolical;' and that it could not be complied with. He concluded his answer with the assertion, that "Not one man will the State of Missouri furnish to carry on such an unholy crusade."

Jackson, through General Frost, was raising an army. According to his own words these troops could not be for the support of the national government; therefore his army must be against it.

As soon as General Harney was gone, Captain Lyon determined to strike a blow that would check the rising of the State Guard in the interest of Governor Jackson; for he had reasons to think that it was time to act. By order of the governor, the United States arsenal at Liberty had been seized on April 20, 1861. Moreover, two of the avenues in Camp Jackson were called "Davis" and "Beauregard," in honor of two of the most noted Confederate leaders. Captain Lyon also suspected that the camp was being fortified with ordnance taken by the Confederates from Federal arsenals; for it was said that boxes marked "marble," which had been hauled there from the river, contained cannon and mortars, and that barrels of ammunition had been sent with them.

To satisfy himself as to the truth of these reports, the captain determined to turn spy and reconnoiter the camp himself. He borrowed a dress, shawl, and bonnet of a friend, and disguised himself in this female attire. Accompanied by Captain J. J. Witzig as guide, he entered a carriage and rode around Camp Jackson unsuspected. What he saw and heard was sufficient to rouse him to immediate action.

After he was convinced of the treasonable intent of Jackson and Frost, Lyon held a consultation with the committee of safety, and acquainted them with his design to seize the camp. They all approved it, except Glover and How.

On May 10, General Frost, learning of the plan, wrote to Captain Lyon, denying that he had any hostile intentions toward the government, or any design on the arsenal. Lyon responded that Frost's command was regarded as hostile toward the government of the United States; that Frost was in open communication with the Confederacy, and was receiving supplies and munitions of war from it; that he had refused to disperse his forces in obedience to the proclamation of the President; and that the immediate necessities of state policy and warfare, and the obligations imposed upon himself by his instructions, compelled him to demand immediate surrender. The only promise he

General Nathaniel Lyon.

made was that the prisoners should be humanely and kindly treated.

General Frost could not misunderstand this communication. Before it reached him, however, Lyon and Blair had started out with between six and seven thousand well-armed troops, and twenty pieces of artillery, and were on their way from the barracks to Camp Jackson.

As told in the St. Louis newspapers of the time, the soldiers rapidly surrounded the camp, planting their batteries upon all the heights overlooking it. Long files of men were stationed in platoons on every side, and a picket guard was established, covering an area of two hundred yards. The guards, with fixed bayonets and muskets at half cock, were instructed to allow none to pass within the limit thus taken up.

By this time an immense crowd of people had assembled in the vicinity. They came in carriages, buggies, cars, and baggage wagons, on horseback, and on foot. Some had arms, as is supposed, with the intention of assisting the State troops, but the careful planting of the guard prevented them from entering the camp. The hills in the neighborhood were covered with people, and hundreds of women and children mingled with the throngs, little dreaming of danger.

On receiving Captain Lyon's demand for surrender, General Frost called a hasty consultation of the officers of his staff. Resistance was clearly out of the question, and they decided to surrender. The State troops were therefore made prisoners of war, but were offered their release on condition that they would take an oath to support the Constitution of the United States, and not to take up arms against the government. All but eight or ten preferred to remain in confinement.

The prisoners, about eight hundred

in number, were formed in line for marching to the arsenal. The brigade was headed by General Frost and his staff on horseback, and with colors flying and drums beating, they marched to a wood that skirted the road.

About half past five, the prisoners of war left the grove and entered the road. The United States soldiers inclosed them in a single file stretched along each side of the line. When a halt was made, large crowds of people pressed forward, hooting and jeering.

Then some German soldiers at the head of the column lost their temper and opened fire. Fortunately, no one was injured, and the soldiers who had discharged their guns were promptly put under arrest.

Hardly was tranquillity restored, however, when volley after volley was heard from the extreme rear, and men, women, and children were seen flying frantically from the place. While running, many were shot down, and the wounded and dying made the late beautiful field look like a battle ground. The number of killed and wounded was about twenty-five, including two women and one child. The soldiers who fired claimed that they were first attacked with stones, and fired upon by the crowd. The firing was done by Boernstein's company, and at the command of an officer.

Night closed in, and hid the ghastly horrors of the scene. A German regiment took possession of Camp Jackson, and the prisoners were conducted to the barracks.

The feeling in the city that night was intense. The most frequented streets and avenues were thronged with citizens in the highest state of excitement. Loud huzzas and occasional shots were heard in various localities. All public resorts were closed at dark, and the windows of private dwellings were fastened, in the fear of a general riot; but the police succeeded in preventing any serious outbreak.

Next day, General Frost and his command were all paroled and set at liberty, with the exception of Captain Emmet McDonald, who refused to take the oath required.

XXXVI.

A GOVERNOR'S FLIGHT.

MAY 12, 1861, two days after Camp Jackson was taken, Brigadier-General W. S. Harney, commandant of the department, returned to St. Louis from Washington. He approved of what Lyon had done, but issued a proclamation intended to conciliate all parties.

Immediately after the capture of Camp Jackson, however, the Legislature passed a law, called the "Military Bill," which provided for arming the militia. This law was cause for a second proclamation from General Harney. He denounced the Military Bill as "an indirect secession ordinance, ignoring even the forms resorted to by other States, and unconstitutional and void." But he declared no intention to use the soldiers under his command, unless forced to do so.

Under the new military bill the governor appointed Sterling Price major general of the State Guard. This man was a former Congressman, an ex-governor of the State, and one of the heroes of the Mexican War.

In order to preserve the public peace, Harney and Price held a conference in St. Louis on May 21. As a result of this meeting, both signed an agreement, by which the management of the State Guard was turned over to General Price, under direction of Governor

General Sterling Price.

Jackson; and General Harney publicly declared that he had no desire to make any military movement "which might otherwise create excitement and jealousies." On the same day, General Harney issued a proclamation to the people of Missouri, setting forth the compact, and stating that the forces of both the State and the Federal governments were pledged to bring about peace.

General Harney's actions were not approved by the national government, and he was relieved from the command of the post. Captain Lyon succeeded him. It was well that he did, for the general had already taken steps for removing the Federal troops from Missouri. Governor Jackson and General Price, in accordance with the arrangement, disbanded the State troops at Jefferson City, and ordered them home to drill and receive military instruction.

The removal of General Harney and the appointment of Captain Lyon precipitated affairs. With the views Jackson held, he would in any case have gone with the Confederate States. It is quite probable, however, that under different circumstances Price would have remained what he first declared himself to be, a Union man. He never favored secession, and only his loyalty to Missouri, according to his own peculiar views, forced him into the Confederate army.

On June 11, 1861, there was a second conference between the officers of State and Federal governments. This interview was held at the Planters House in St. Louis. General Nathaniel Lyon, Colonel Francis P. Blair, and Major H. A. Conant represented the United States, while Governor C. F. Jackson, General Sterling Price, and Colonel Thomas L. Snead represented the State. An eyewitness of the scene says, —

"Lyon advanced into the room, a little, red-haired, precise, positive, plain man. He sat down and crossed one leg over the other stiffly, and his face was serious and stern. He spoke each word separate from the other, pronouncing the little words, like *my* and *to*, with as much emphasis as the longer words. He raised his right arm automatically as the conversation proceeded, and brought it down with a jerk, extending the forefinger, yet never speaking higher or lower than at first.

"'I shall take small part in this conference,' said Lyon. 'Mr. Blair is familiar with this question, and knows the views of my government, and has its full confidence. What he has to say will have my support.'

"Yet in half an hour he took the case out of Blair's mouth and advanced to the front, and Frank Blair was as dumb as Lyon had been."

Governor Jackson's object was to prevent the enlistment of men in his State to help force the Confederate States back into the Union. His last attempt was to get Lyon to agree that neither side should recruit troops in Missouri. Shaking his head, Lyon rose and in his measured, even, earnest tones said,—

"Rather than agree that my government shall concede to your government one iota of authority as to

one man to be recruited, one inch of soil to be divided in allegiance or neutralized between my government and your government, I will see you, Sir (pointing to Price), and you, Sir (pointing to Jackson), and myself, and all of us, under the sod!" Then taking out his watch he glanced at it, and added: "You shall have safe conduct out of my lines for one hour. Meanwhile, you can get dinner. It is now three o'clock."

The subject was beyond further discussion. Jackson, Price, and Snead took a hurried dinner, and left St. Louis on an express train. Fearing that Lyon would catch them before they reached Jefferson City, they burned bridges and cut telegraph communications behind them.

Next day, Governor Jackson issued a proclamation calling into active service fifty thousand militiamen "for the purpose of repelling invasion, and for the protection of the lives, liberty, and property of the citizens of the State." With this act the civil war in Missouri began.

No man was ever more decisive or quick to act than General Lyon. On June 13, the day after Governor Jackson's proclamation, he started up the Missouri River with steamboats carrying fifteen hundred soldiers. He was accompanied by Colonel Francis P. Blair, who commanded the First Missouri regiment of volunteer infantry.

Jackson and Price were advised of their approach, and at once left the capital on the steamboat "White Cloud."

On Saturday, June 15, at three o'clock P.M., the forces of General Lyon reached Jefferson City, disembarked, and took possession of the town. But the governor had gone. Missouri was without a chief executive until July 30, 1861, when the State convention appointed Hon. Hamilton R. Gamble to fill the office. He is known in history as the war governor of Missouri.

XXXVII.

A HERO'S DEATH.

ON June 16, General Lyon left Jefferson City in command of Colonel Henry Boernstein, and went up the river to Boonville with most of his troops. The wisdom of this prompt action may be seen from the fact that Price and Jackson were rapidly raising an army. The conference between Lyon and Jackson, with their associates, was on June 11. On the 12th, Jackson issued his call for fifty thousand men. On the 14th, Jackson and Price left Jefferson City, and on the 16th they had collected at Boonville an army of three or four thousand men. A week's hesitation or delay would have given them an overwhelming force.

General Price was at this time taken seriously ill, and left on the "White Cloud" for his residence in Chariton County. Governor Jackson and Colonel John S. Marmaduke, a West Point graduate, were left to resist the advance of Lyon and Blair. Their men were poorly armed, equipped, and disciplined to meet the United States forces, and less than half of them were at all prepared for immediate service; but these "were full of fight," and insisted on being led against the enemy. Halfway from Rocheport to Boonville the two armies met, and Lyon began the conflict with a few rounds from Totten's artillery. The State troops were driven from their position again and again, but they behaved gallantly for raw recruits. Lyon at last forced them from the field, however, and they fled to Boonville.

According to the best accounts to be had, the United States forces lost two killed, nine wounded, and one missing; their opponents had two killed and several wounded. This first conflict in Missouri was only a skirmish, and a year later would hardly have been noticed in an official report.

On June 17, General Lyon occupied Boonville, and issued a proclamation declaring that he intended to use the force under his command, for no other purpose than the maintenance of the authority of the general government, and for the protection of the rights and property of all law-abiding citizens.

When Jackson fled from Boonville, he went to Arrow Rock, in Saline County, and from there to Syracuse, where he gathered about him a force of sixteen hundred men. Lyon sent a Federal force to capture him, but Jackson and his men escaped to southwest Missouri.

On July 5, 1861, Colonel Franz Sigel, who had entered Jasper County, met the force under Governor Jackson, and Generals Rains and Parsons, near Carthage. After a conflict of two hours it became dark. Sigel fell back into Carthage, and then to Sarcoxie. His loss was twenty-four killed and forty-five wounded, but Jackson's loss was fully as great.

In the mean while, General Price had gone from his home to Lexington, and then to Arkansas, where he induced the Confederate McCulloch to march north to

Jackson's aid. For some time after this, southwestern Missouri was held by the followers of Jackson, while the northern and eastern parts of the State were mostly controlled by Union men. Each party was busily engaged in raising and equipping troops.

Governor Jackson, after a visit to Richmond, issued a proclamation, in which he declared Missouri a SOVEREIGN, FREE, AND INDEPENDENT REPUBLIC, with full power to levy war, conclude peace, contract alliances, establish commerce, and do all other acts and things which an independent State may do. This was early in August. In October, Jackson's followers in the General Assembly met and adopted measures, on the strength of which Missouri was formally admitted to the Confederacy. To avoid confusion, however, the Jackson State troops may be called Confederates even before this time.

On July 6, 1861, the authorities at Washington created what was called the "Western Department" in the army. That is, the armies in a certain number of States and Territories were to be commanded by one general. The Western Department included the State of Illinois and all the States and Territories west of the Mississippi and east of the Rocky Mountains, including New Mexico. Major-General John C. Fremont was appointed to command the department, with headquarters at St. Louis.

Fremont was a prominent man at that time. He was a son-in-law of the late Senator Thomas H. Benton, and had made himself so famous as an explorer that he is known in history as the "Path Finder." He was also the Republican candidate for President in 1856. When the war broke out, he was in Europe; but he hastened to America, and on the 26th of July reached St. Louis.

Meanwhile, the hero of the war in Missouri, General Nathaniel Lyon, was in the field guarding southern Missouri, ready, if need be, to lay his own body "under the sod" for his country. He held his command in the vicinity of Springfield, which was seriously threatened by a much greater force under Price, McCulloch, Pearce, and McBride.

Toward the last of July, General Lyon was informed of the concentration of Southern troops at Cassville. He determined to go out and meet them with his army. Altogether, he had five thousand five hundred infantry, four hundred cavalry, and eighteen pieces of artillery; but of this slender force he was compelled to leave enough to guard the city. The Confederate army under General Rains was met by Lyon at Dug Springs, August 2. The fight was stubborn, but at last Rains was forced to beat a retreat. His loss was eighty killed and wounded, while Lyon had eight killed and thirty wounded.

After a short pursuit, General Lyon returned to Springfield, which point he reached August 6. Realizing the overwhelming numbers which were confronting him, he had repeatedly called on General Fremont for reinforcements. But from rumors that reached his ears Fremont supposed that Cairo and Bird Point were threatened; and he therefore decided not to help Lyon, whose small army of less than six thousand was confronted by one twice as large, and constantly increasing.

With a fleet of eight boats Fremont steamed down the river to Bird Point with all his army. No enemy threatened the place, and it is probable that Pillow had intentionally decoyed him thither to prevent his reinforcing General Lyon. Fremont steamed back again without having seen an enemy, and many historians doubt if Bird Point was at any time in danger.

The combined armies of Price and McCulloch marched toward Springfield, and on August 9 they reached Wilson Creek. Here they encamped, intending to march against Lyon at nine next morning. It was their original intention to march on the town that night, but a storm threatened, and as the darkness was intense, McCulloch countermanded the order.

The night was not too dark or stormy, however, for General Lyon. Left to his fate by his commander, he determined to strike a blow that would paralyze the ever-increasing enemy, if it cost him his life. Apprised of the advance of the Confederates, he left Springfield at five o'clock in the afternoon, marched through darkness and storm, and came in sight of the enemy's camp fires at one o'clock in the morning. He halted his men, and they lay on their arms until daylight, and then quickly formed.

The morning attack by Lyon and Sigel was a complete surprise to the Confederates, whose outposts were quickly driven in. Totten's battery opened a terrible fire, and the forests and hills seemed ablaze. Union skirmishers were thrown forward, and Lyon's forces advanced, the firing increasing until the column commanded by him was warmly engaged. The constant rolling volleys, the deafening echoes, shouts, and groans made a terrible din. At times, Lyon's column was wrapped in smoke.

The sun rose and looked down on the fearful conflict. The fields and woods were covered with slain, and still the battle raged. Sometimes the Union forces seemed on the verge of victory, then overwhelming odds drove them back, in spite of all Lyon's skill and valor.

In the mean while the troops under Sigel had been put to flight. Their guns were heard over the hill for a while, then became silent, and every one asked, —

"Where is Sigel?"

While endeavoring to rally the Union lines which had been thrown into confusion, on the left of Totten's battery, General Lyon was wounded in the leg and head, and his horse was killed. Though the wounds were slight, he bled profusely. He bound a handkerchief about his head, and Major Sturgis dismounted one of his orderlies, and gave his horse to the general.

Some Iowa troops had lost their colonel, and were in confusion. They were ordered to charge the advancing Confederates.

"We have no leader," cried some one.

"Come on! I will lead you!" shouted General Lyon, and waving his hat he once more shouted, "Come on!"

It was near nine o'clock; and Lyon, for the first time doubtful, yet brave to the last, led in the attack. He rode his horse between the First Kansas and First Iowa regiments, waving his sword, and shouting and urging the soldiers on to the conflict. He wore a white felt hat and his old captain's uniform. He looked stunned and white, yet brave and defiant, and shouted repeatedly, —

"Come on!"

The blood was trickling down one side of his face. He had gone about one hundred yards, when a bullet struck him in the breast, inflicting a fatal wound. As he slowly dismounted and fell into the arms of his bodyguard, he gasped, —

"Lehman, I'm going!"

Captain Herron asked him if he was much hurt.

"No," he answered. But he probably did not know what he said; for he died almost immediately.

Sturgis took command, and drove the Confederates back four hundred yards; but, in the end, the Union forces were compelled to retreat to Rolla. The loss on the Union side was about one thousand, and on the other side much greater. The conflict at Wilson Creek was the first great battle in Missouri.

General Lyon's body was first buried at Springfield, but was afterwards reinterred with great military honors at Eastford, Connecticut, his old home.

XXXVIII.

WAR IN THE NORTH.

WHILE war was raging in the south and southwest, north Missouri for a time enjoyed comparative peace. Union troops were constantly being enlisted, and detachments of them were stationed at various towns. One regiment, commanded by Colonel David Moore, was posted at Athens, in Clark County.

At the same time, too, some soldiers were being enlisted on the other side; among them was a regiment under Colonel Martin E. Greene, who determined to drive the Union troops out of Athens.

About sunrise, August 5, 1861, Greene's advance guard attacked Moore's pickets, and drove them in. Then the main force in two wings came up, and the conflict became general.

It was a fight between Missourians, for there were scarcely a dozen men from any other State on the field. Many of them had been friends and neighbors. Even fathers, sons, and brothers were arrayed against one another. Colonel David Moore himself had a son, William, who was a captain under the Confederate Colonel Greene, and who fought against his father in this conflict. It is said that as Greene was marching on Athens, some of his officers remarked in Captain Moore's hearing, —

"Now, boys, we'll have old Moore without firing a gun." To which the son quickly responded, —

"No, you won't. If you think dad won't fight, you are mistaken. I know the old man too well."

His father did fight, and sent the son, his colonel, and their men flying in confusion, with considerable loss. The fight at Athens, though really little more than a skirmish, was important as being the first in which brother grappled with brother in north Missouri.

Colonel Mulligan of the Union forces had fortified Lexington, in Lafayette County, just south of the river, and thither the Confederates under Price were moving. Greene and all the forces of the Confederates from the northern part of the State were also moving in that direction. Mulligan threw up intrenchments on Masonic College Hill, an eminence which comprises about fifteen acres adjoining the city on the northeast, and overlooking the Missouri River.

On September 12, 1861, Price attacked the Union works. He met with a strong resistance, but by rolling forward hempen bales, soaked to keep them from taking fire, he steadily advanced. Mulligan, like Lyon, had appealed in vain for reinforcements, and after a siege of fifty-two hours, he surrendered on the 20th. The conflict had been stubborn, but the loss was not great. Forty Union men were killed, and one hundred and twenty wounded, while the Confederate loss was twenty killed and seventy-five wounded. Price, however, captured many arms and great military stores in the town.

On September 27, General Fremont, with twenty thousand men, advanced toward southwest Missouri; and on the 30th General Price marched south toward Arkansas, leaving a garrison of five hundred in possession of Lexington. Only four days later, the town was reoccupied by the Union forces.

This left the northern part of the State in peace until 1862. Early that year, Colonel Jo Porter, knowing that there were many sympathizers with the Southern cause north of the Missouri, crossed the river with about eighty men for the purpose of rallying a Confederate force. Reinforcements flocked to his standard so rapidly that if they could have gone south of the river, they would have added very materially to Price's army; but the country was held by Union troops, and Porter was compelled to fight many battles.

Colonel Lipscomb, with about four hundred and fifty militia, attacked Porter's men in June at Cherry Grove, in Schuyler County, and drove them into Knox County. Then followed a skirmish at Pierces Mill, then one at Florida.

Though Porter was nearly all the time on the retreat, he was rapidly recruiting. Poindexter, another Confederate, was raising troops in the northwestern part of the State, while Porter was at work in the northeast, and it was the intention of these two officers to unite their forces, and then join Price.

Colonel Odon Guitar of the Missouri State militia attacked Porter at Moores Mill in Callaway County, July 28, 1862. Guitar being reinforced by Lieutenant-Colonel Shaffer, Porter was driven from the thick woods in which he was posted, and retreated north.

Colonel John H. McNiel was at this time at Mexico, in Audrain County. With detachments of the Ninth Missouri State militia under Captain Leonard, and one hundred of the "Merrills Horse" under Lieutenant-Colonel Shaffer, he gave chase to Porter. Through Honeywell and Shelbina, and into Lewis County, McNiel pressed the Confederates. Porter attacked a force of militia in a brick house at Newark, and after a sharp fight captured them, with about three hundred stands of arms. The prisoners were paroled. McNiel was close at hand, so Porter hastily left town and marched toward Memphis, Scotland County.

He marched to within three miles of the town, and then, finding McNiel too close in the rear, suddenly turned southwest toward Kirksville, in Adair County. McNiel's army, by forced marches, came within a few miles of the Confederates on the evening of August 5, 1862, and went into camp.

At early dawn, the Union forces were in the saddle. Lieutenant J. G. Jamison, with Company B, Ninth Missouri State militia, started in advance, and soon came upon the smoldering camp fires of the enemy. They pressed on, and about eleven o'clock, when three or four miles from Kirksville, they came in sight of a few of Porter's rear guard who were engaged in tearing up a bridge. Jamison opened fire on them, and wounded one man; and the others fled.

In half an hour, the advance of the Union forces were within a quarter of a mile of the town, and were forming in line of battle on an open meadow east of Kirksville, when the main body came up. McNiel and his staff rode down a slight descent toward a cornfield, when some shots were fired at them, and drove them back.

Not a Confederate was in sight. The quiet little village seemed uninhabited. A cow was peacefully grazing on the common, and a calf could be seen sporting in the yard of a house near by. The Union line was just west of the two-story house of Mr. Oldham, which is still standing.

Three or four puffs of smoke issued from behind a wood pile in the east part of the town, and some musket balls flew over the heads of the Union troops. One of the balls struck a window sill in the Oldham house. McNiel was still at a loss to locate the position of the enemy, so he called for volunteers to ride forward in the hope of rousing them. A lieutenant of the Merrills Horse, with ten men, rode out from the line.

At the word "Forward!" the lieutenant and his brave followers dashed down under the hill on the northeast part of the town, and were off like the wind. For a moment they were lost to view. Then came the rapid discharge of firearms, and rattling volleys. The men were seen to ride past a cornfield, nearer to the town. Every one held his breath, expecting that the whole band would be annihilated; but a moment later they were seen galloping back with not a saddle emptied. Right back into the ranks they flew. Then one horse, which had been shot through, sank dead, and a wounded cavalryman fell fainting from his saddle.

The howitzers meanwhile had been playing on the town with little effect except to kill the calf that was playing in the yard. On the return of the lieutenant and his cavalrymen, McNiel said, —

"Advance and take the town, house by house, and keep yourselves in line as well as possible."

The order was given to march, and the enemy opened fire. A wide expanse of meadow had to be crossed, in the face of raking volleys from the Confederates. The Union soldiers crossed the common, and drove the enemy from house to house and from street to street until Porter's forces were pushed into the wood west of the town.

The Confederate loss was about three hundred killed and wounded, and two hundred made prisoners. McNiel had eight killed and a large number wounded.

On the 7th of August, the day after the battle, McNiel had sixteen of the prisoners shot for having been paroled and again taking up arms against their country. On the 8th, he marched his force to Macon City. Meanwhile Porter and the remnant of his army, about twenty-five hundred men, crossed the Chariton at Sloans Point, and hurried westward, hoping to form a junction with Poindexter.

Colonel Guitar, with a considerable force and some pieces of artillery, came upon the Confederates at Comptons Ferry and drove them back toward the Chariton again. They crossed at Sees Ford, and there made a stand against Guitar, who did not cross the river.

Three hours after McNiel went down the road to Macon City, Porter's army crossed the road in his rear at Blanket Grove. After a little more insignificant skirmishing, he disbanded all his men, except his original company of eighty, with which number he crossed the river and joined Price.

XXXIX.

ORDER NUMBER ELEVEN.

THERE were many cruel acts during the war, but perhaps the most cruel was what was known as "General Ewing's Special Order Number Eleven." There have been several excuses offered for this order, but before one can understand either it, or the excuses offered for it, a sketch of the war is essential.

Fremont was succeeded by Hunter in command of the Western Department November 2, 1861. Five days later, Grant defeated the Confederates at Belmont:

Price, McCulloch, and Van Dorn, having concentrated their forces at a place called Elk Horn Tavern (or Pea Ridge) in Arkansas, were attacked by General Curtis on March 6, 1862. The Confederates were defeated with heavy losses, General McCulloch being killed, and Price wounded.

At Springfield, Missouri, in January, 1863, and at Cape Girardeau the following April, General Marmaduke of the Confederate army was repulsed. In August of the same year, the Confederate General Jeff Thompson was captured.

Thus the Confederate forces were nearly all driven out of Missouri during the first two years of the war; but the State was not at peace. The long border warfare carried on between 1856 and 1861 was now bearing terrible fruit. The jayhawkers and guerrillas, who began to plunder and kill four years before the war, doubled their acts of violence after it had begun.

They became widely known as guerrillas on one side and militia plunderers on the other. Of course, however, all the militia were not plunderers. Many thousands of the bravest and best soldiers in the Union army were from the Missouri militia. But there were two or three border regiments, composed mostly of men who had been jayhawkers, who did but little fighting, and a good deal of pillaging from persons supposed to be in sympathy with the people of the South. On the Confederate side, there were large bands of guerrillas and bushwhackers, who carried on a war of plunder and extermination.

The last named were under such notorious chiefs as William Quantrell, George Todd, and Bill Anderson. Their usual mode of warfare was to lie at the roadside in a thicket, and fire on small parties of soldiers as they passed.

In 1863, Quantrell's guerrillas seemed to be the only Confederates capable of holding their position in Missouri. The chief would concentrate his force in a few hours, and strike a paralyzing blow at his enemy; then the band would scatter and vanish as if the earth had swallowed them up. The secret of their disappearance was that in Jackson, Bates, Cass, and Clay counties the guerrillas had many friends, who evidently sheltered them and concealed them from their pursuers.

The object of the guerrillas was to harass the Union

soldiers and prevent them from concentrating against Price. The Union officers discovered, that, while they could keep the Confederate armies out of the State, it was impossible to drive out the guerrillas.

"They live like rats in holes in the ground," one officer declared after a long and useless chase.

The many terrible and daring deeds of the guerrillas would fill a large book. It is said that one of them, disguised as an old woman, rode into Independence on horseback when the town was filled with soldiers. The long riding skirt hid his boots, and all went well until he started to leave the town. Just as he was riding past one of the first sentries, a sudden puff of wind lifted his skirts, and displayed his boots and spurs.

"It's a man! It's a man!" cried one of the sentries.

Being discovered, the guerrilla made no further effort to disguise himself. Throwing himself astride the horse, he took the rein in his teeth, and a revolver in each hand, and started at full speed away from the town.

"Halt! halt! halt!" shouted the sentry.

As the guerrilla paid no heed to the command, the sentry fired at him, the ball whizzing close to the ear of the fleeing man. The outside pickets were roused by the firing; but, seeing a woman riding furiously toward them, they hesitated for a moment to shoot.

That moment's delay was fatal. The disguised guerrilla fired a stream of shots from each revolver, mortally wounding two of the guards, while the third saved himself by leaping into a thicket. The guerrilla escaped.

With all the guerrillas Quantrell could gather (about five hundred) he marched to Lawrence, Kansas, burned the town, and killed a number of men, women, and children (August 13, 1863).

So terrible a scourge had these bands become, that it was thought necessary to resort to some extreme measures in order to rid the country of them. General Thomas Ewing was at this time in command of the military district of which Kansas City formed the center. On the 25th day of August, 1863, he issued an order called SPECIAL ORDER NUMBER ELEVEN.

This was to the effect that all persons living in Cass, Jackson, and Bates counties, Missouri, and in that part of Vernon included in the "district of the border," were ordered to leave their houses within fifteen days, unless they lived within one mile of the limits of Independence, Hickman Mills, Pleasant Hill, or Harrisonville, or in that part of Kaw Township, Jackson County, north of Brush Creek and west of the Big Blue, including Kansas City and Westport. Those who could prove their loyalty were to be granted permission to live at some military post, but those who could not were to leave the district. All grain and hay found in the fields were to be taken to military stations. All products of the farm not thus removed by the 9th of September were to be destroyed.

This was an act more cruel in many cases than taking life, for thousands of helpless women and children were made homeless. Eviction followed close upon the order. The guerrilla warfare which had raged for two years on the border had driven away many of the people in these counties, and this order entirely depopulated them. Many were the scenes of suffering and wretchedness caused by the evictions. These have been rendered famous by Mr. George C. Bingham, "the Missouri artist," in his great painting entitled "Order No. 11."

A soldier who was forced to drive the poor people from their homes, among other incidents, describes the following, —

"We were sent to remove a family living in Cass County. Unfortunately, our commanding officer was an unprincipled, brutal fellow, who was nearly always under the influence of liquor. We reached the house shortly after dark.

"There were no men about the place. Two frightened women and four or five children were the only occupants of the house. We surrounded the building, and the lieutenant went to the door and rapped on it with his sword hilt. A woman came to the window and asked, —

"'What do you want?'

"'Why haven't you moved according to orders?' the officer demanded.

"'We are all sick, and there are no men here,' she answered.

"The officer swore some ugly oaths, and said they should be moved out at once. The women begged him to let them remain until daylight. We interceded for them, and the lieutenant finally agreed that they might stay; but he broke down the door, and searched the house for arms and men, swearing he would kill every man he found.

"The search proved fruitless. When it was over, the half-drunken officer stood in the door abusing the cowering women, who, pale and trembling, crept back to the bed, and remained mute. While our intoxicated lieutenant was making terrible threats, there appeared at one of the windows the sad face of a child. She was not over five years of age, but had the thoughtful demeanor of an adult. With her elbow resting on the window sill, and her head leaning on her hand, she gazed upon us. Her little pinched face was very pale. Her large, tearless eyes were sad, and she heaved such sighs and looked so sorrowful that she would have melted any heart that was human.

"I could no more look on that child and restrain my tears than I could quit breathing. I called the attention of several of my comrades to her, and not an eye that beheld her was dry. Next morning we drove the family away, burned their house, and destroyed all their property. Heaven only knows what the fate of those women and children was."

The counties included in General Ewing's Special Order Number Eleven were almost completely devastated. For years after the war, only blackened chimneys and abandoned orchards remained to tell where happy homes had once been. What became of all the people driven away from their possessions, is not known.

Nearly every one, probably, has read of the eviction of the Acadians, as described by Longfellow in his beautiful poem, "Evangeline." Scores of stories fully as sad as "Evangeline" might be written of Ewing's Order Number Eleven.

Fortunately, some of the soldiers sent to enforce the order were honest and kind. In one instance, when the women and children had been driven from the house, and the building set on fire, a woman went to a soldier who had shown more of a gentlemanly spirit than the others, and said, —

"There is three hundred and thirty dollars in gold in the front room."

"What part of the room is it in?" he asked.

"The southeast corner, under the carpet. The bureau is over it."

The flames were roaring about the building, the room was already full of smoke, and blazes were licking the sides of the door, when the soldier ran into the house.

The upper story was already ablaze, and bits of burning wood were dropping down from above. The woman was sorry she had told him of the money, for it seemed as if it would be impossible for him to escape from the burning building. But a few moments later, he leaped from the flames, and, leading her aside, placed the money in her hands.

"Take it," whispered the noble soldier. "Don't let the others know it; for there are some who would take it from you."

"Won't you take some of it?" she began.

"Not a cent. You will need it all before this is over."

Such heroic deeds lighten the darkest page in the history of Missouri. War develops the true nature of men. Those naturally brutal are made more so by it, while those brave and gentle become heroes.

If General Ewing's Order Number Eleven was intended to end the guerrilla warfare, it was a miserable failure. The ruined district became a great desert which the guerrillas made their rendezvous, and their depredations became more terrible than they had ever been before.

XL.

END OF THE WAR.

DURING the years 1863 and 1864 there were many skirmishes in Missouri, but no great battles. Large Confederate armies were kept out of the State, but the Union forces found it impossible to keep down the prowling bands of bushwhackers and guerrillas. Their depredations made it necessary to maintain a standing army in the State.

For the most part, military operations in 1864 degenerated into a savage guerrilla warfare. The greatest outrage committed by the Confederate outlaws was the robbing of Centralia, September 27, 1864, and the massacre of a large number of Federal soldiers.

Bill Anderson, with about four hundred guerrillas, went to the farm of Mr. M. G. Singleton, a few miles from Centralia, on the night of September 26. Early next morning, small scouting parties proceeded to the village and began taking horses and robbing stores.

An hour or so later, Anderson and the others also went to Centralia, which was on what was then the North Missouri Railroad, — now a part of the Wabash system. About eleven o'clock the stagecoach from Columbia arrived at the village. The guerrillas surrounded it with cocked revolvers, crying, —

"Out with your pocketbooks!"

The passengers were robbed, and the horses taken from the stage. About half past eleven the train from St. Louis came in sight. Bill Anderson placed his men along the railroad; and, as the train approached the depot, they began throwing ties across the track.

There were twenty-three soldiers on the train. Most of them were on sick furloughs, going to their homes in north Missouri or Iowa. A big sergeant glanced out of the car window as the train began to slow up, and cried, —

"There is Bill Anderson, boys. Now prepare to die."

He drew a revolver, and would have defended himself, had he not been dissuaded from doing so, on account of the women and children on board. The train stopped, and the guerrillas robbed the passengers. The soldiers were taken from the cars, marched to the town, and formed in a line. At the word "Fire!" Anderson and three or four others began shooting them. Several tried to escape, and others begged for their lives. One man ran under the depot platform, but the building was set on fire, and as he came out he was shot in the head.

Having killed all the soldiers, robbed the town, and burned the depot and train, Anderson and his men retired to the woods about six or eight miles west of Centralia.

Major Johnson, of the Thirty-ninth Missouri U. S. volunteers, entered the town with about one hundred and seventy-five raw recruits a short time after Anderson had left. Incensed by the barbarous acts of the guerrillas, Johnson determined to follow and attack them with his inferior force. It is said, that, as he was leaving Centralia for that purpose, a young girl sprang before him, and, seizing his horse's bridle, begged him with tears in her eyes not to go. He heeded not her warning, but led his soldiers across the prairie to battle.

An hour later, Major Johnson and one hundred and thirty-eight of his men were lying dead on the prairie, and the remainder of his command was flying northward to Renick, a small town ten miles from Centralia.

* * * * * * * *

Early in September, 1864, it became evident that General Sterling Price, who was in the northern part of Arkansas, intended to invade Missouri. General Rosecrans, who was now in command of the Union forces in Missouri, had not soldiers enough to repel so large an army as Price was reported to have. The War Department realized the situation of Rosecrans, and sent General A. J. Smith, with six thousand men, to reinforce him.

About the middle of September, Price entered Missouri with a considerable army, and marched on Pilot

Knob, where a brigade of Union troops under General H. S. Ewing was stationed. Ewing resisted two of Price's assaults, but finally was driven from Pilot Knob, and fled northwest. His men marched sixty miles in thirty-nine hours. They then reached the Southeastern Railroad at Harrison, where they hoped to get a few hours' rest, but were disappointed. The Confederate General Jo Shelby had been close at their heels, and here he overtook them and attacked them furiously. Ewing's exhausted troops defended themselves for thirty hours, and then reinforcements from Rolla came and drove Shelby away.

Price, meanwhile, advanced boldly in a northerly direction, driving the small detachments of Union troops before him. For some time it was a matter of doubt which the Confederate general intended to attack, Jefferson City or St. Louis. He marched to Richwoods, within forty miles of St. Louis, in order to draw the Union generals in that direction. Then he made a sudden flank movement, and began a rapid march toward Jefferson City, burning the bridges behind him as he went; and he reached the place before his pursuers could overtake him.

The Union officers, however, were not outgeneraled by Price. Some of the best in the State believed from the first that the wily Confederate intended to seize the State capital. General Brown, with a small force of Union troops, was stationed there, and General Fisk, with such force as he could gather about him, hastened to his aid. General Rosecrans ordered all the enrolled militia, and such other troops as could be spared, to march at once to Jefferson City; and General A. J. Smith, with about six thousand Union soldiers, was close after Price even as he marched on the capital.

When the Confederate army reached the Moreau River, five miles below the capital, it encountered the outposts of the Union army under Brown and Fisk. After a slight skirmish, Price crossed the river and advanced on the city. But the forces of Brown and Fisk, with the aid of citizens from all the country round, had thrown up breastworks and planted batteries, which it would take the Confederates too long to capture. General Price found himself about to be caught in a trap, between Brown and Fisk on one side, and Smith on the other; so he marched on westward.

Though retreating, Price was not defeated. General Jo Shelby, one of his officers, captured the town of Glasgow, and Price himself defeated Curtis at the Little Blue Creek, October 20. On the 23d, however, the Union cavalry defeated Price's rear guard and drove the Confederates out of Independence, Jackson County.

From Independence, General Price retreated south into Arkansas. His retreat was well conducted, and was almost one continuous fight from Jefferson City to the Arkansas line. During that retreat two notorious guerrillas, George Todd and Bill Anderson, were killed.

Except for skirmishes with bands of guerrillas, the departure of Price from Missouri ended the war in that State. And only about six months later came the surrender of Lee and other generals, after which there was peace throughout the nation.

XLI.

THE IRONCLAD OATH.

FOR four years Missouri had been under military government. The people had become thoroughly tired of it, and at the same time there was a demand for a change in the State constitution. Even before the war ended, the party in power was anxious to bring some amendments before the people.

At the November election in 1864, the people chose delegates to a State constitutional convention. The members of this body — sixty-six in number — met in the Mercantile Library Hall, in the city of St. Louis, January 6, 1865. After passing an ordinance abolishing slavery, they framed what was known as the "Drake constitution," so called from the name of their vice president. The disfranchising portions of the instrument were called the "Draconian code."

The third section of the Drake constitution provided that no one who had ever participated in the Rebellion against the United States, or had given aid, comfort, countenance, or support to persons engaged in it, or who had ever sympathized with the cause, or with those engaged in the cause, should be permitted to hold office or vote at any election.

Section five required that every one who wished to vote or hold office should first make oath that he was familiar with the third section of the constitution, and had never violated any of its provisions. This was commonly called the "ironclad oath," or "test oath."

Not only were disqualifications provided for voters and officeholders, but persons unable to take the oath were prohibited from pursuing certain vocations. No one could practice law, or hold an office in any corporation, or engage as a professor or teacher in any educational institution, public or private school, unless he or she first took the oath; and it was also required of ministers of the gospel, and even of Sunday-school teachers, male and female.

Notwithstanding the many objectionable features of the constitution, it contained some valuable provisions. The section on education was one of the wisest enacted by any convention. One of its provisions, which many regret was not retained in the present constitution, was to the effect that after a certain length of time no one should be permitted to vote who could not write his own name, and read the ballot he proposed to vote.

An election was held June 6, 1865, for the acceptance or rejection of the constitution. All who voted were required to take the "ironclad oath" before doing so. This was very unfair, because it put in force a measure before it really became a law. The constitution was adopted by a majority of less than two thousand.

Some of the best Union men in the State opposed it. General F. P. Blair, the brave soldier who did more, perhaps, than any other man to keep the State in the Union, refused to take the "ironclad oath," and became its bitterest opposer. Like many others, he believed in forgiving an erring brother who had fought on the Confederate side, and in granting him full citizenship, now that the war was over.

It soon became apparent that a division in the Republican party would follow the extreme measures taken by the faction in power, called "Radicals." In 1870, this section of the party renominated Joseph W. McClurg for governor, and the other faction, which was opposed to the Drake constitution, nominated B. Gratz Brown. The latter faction was called the Liberal Republican party. The Democrats had no ticket in the field this year, as their party was too weak to hope for success; but most of them supported Brown and his followers, who promised to repeal the "ironclad oath" and all laws growing out of it. The Liberal Republican ticket was elected, and the objectionable disqualifications were in due time repealed.

There is a story told of an old man who had been disfranchised by the "ironclad oath," which illustrates the feeling entertained by some of the people of Missouri in regard to it. The old man was very sick. His relatives and friends had given up all hope of his recovery, and even the doctor was in despair.

The election of 1870 came off while he was in the most critical stage. The returns were being announced in the village, and some one came into the sick-room and whispered that the Republicans were defeated.

"What is that?" asked the old man who was supposed to be dying.

"The Republicans are defeated, Uncle Isaac — "

"Thank the Lord for that!"

"Don't excite yourself, Uncle. You are very sick, and may not recover if —"

"Recover!" cried the sick man, starting up in bed. "Do you think I'm going to die, when there's a chance

for me to vote again? No; I'll live to see the ironclad oath smashed to flinders."

The old man recovered, and lived to exercise again the rights of citizenship at the polls. He often declared, —

"I couldn't die until Missouri was free from that pernicious ironclad oath!"

XLII.

RESTORATION OF PROSPERITY.

AFTER the year 1864, Missouri was at peace, except for the bands of robbers who were the outgrowth of the guerrillas. For nearly twenty years, these ex-guerrillas or bandits committed the boldest depredations. They plundered village banks in broad daylight, and on one occasion boldly robbed the treasurer of the Kansas City Fair Association in the midst of thousands of people. They stopped railway trains and stagecoaches, and murdered and robbed the passengers. So formidable did these desperate brigands become, that for a while they checked immigration, but, one after another, they were killed or captured, until their number was greatly reduced.

On April 3, 1882, Jesse James, the reputed chief of the Missouri outlaws, was killed at St. Joseph. The deed was committed by two members of his own band, who slew him for the reward offered for him, dead or alive.

On the 9th of June following, a band of masked men who had robbed the Brookfield bank in broad daylight, were captured in Adair County. A few weeks later, Frank James, a brother of Jesse James, surrendered to Governor Crittenden, at Jefferson City. This put an end to an organized banditti in Missouri.

Although the outlaws were a check on the prosperity of the State, they did not by any means wholly restrain it. With the dawn of peace came a revival of business in every line. The soldiers, returning with their back pay and bounties, began to put into cultivation large tracts of wild lands, never before touched with the plow. Some of the returned soldiers became carpenters, some merchants, some school-teachers, and many blacksmiths; but a large majority of them were farmers.

A large number had gone to the war as boys, but returned men, to make homes. New farms were laid out everywhere. Villages almost destroyed during the war were rebuilt, and grew into towns and cities, while new villages sprang up and rapidly became prosperous.

Railroads which had been begun before the war were completed, and new railroads were surveyed and built. People seemed to have gone mad over the building of them. Nearly every county in the State, and in fact nearly every village, held railroad meetings, and offered inducements to railroad companies.

Bonds were recklessly voted for the purpose. Subscriptions by counties and individuals were enormous, and the State would have been bankrupt had not the General Assembly wisely enacted laws preventing counties from voting stock and bonds.

The reckless speculations in this period of prosperity caused men to become dishonest. Many county obligations were voted, for which no railroad was ever built, and it will take years for the people of those districts to pay off such fraudulent debts. Occasionally county officials became corrupt, and were bribed to issue bonds dishonestly. This in one case resulted in the death of the guilty parties. The people of Cass County, exasperated to madness by the fraudulent issue of county bonds, which imposed heavy burdens on the taxpayers without giving them any substantial benefit, resolved on vengeance.

It was charged that the plan had been made by Mr. James C. Cline, the county attorney. Bonds to the amount of several hundred thousand dollars had been issued by the county court, sold, and the money appropriated by the county officials. The accused were indicted and placed under heavy bail for their appearance at court for trial; but many people feared that they would escape just punishment, and when it was learned that some of the parties to the fraud were going to Gunn City on a railway train, a large body of men, masked and armed, gathered at the village.

Gunn City is on the Missouri, Kansas, and Texas Railway, about eleven miles east of Harrisonville, the county seat of Cass County. There were about thirty passengers on board the train, and among them were James C. Cline, Thomas E. Detro, J. C. Stephenson, and General Jo Shelby. Stephenson was one of the judges of the court, and a party to the fraudulent issue of bonds. Cline was the county attorney, and Detro was one of his bondsmen.

When the train entered Gunn City, the engineer saw a great pile of rails, stones, and logs on the track. At the same moment a volley of bullets was fired at the locomotive, and he lost no time in bringing the train to a standstill. Then seventy masked men ran forward, and while some of them drove the engineer and the fireman from their posts, the others kept up a terrible fire on the captured train, causing the innocent passengers to quake with fear.

"Where is Cline? Give us Cline! Come out, Cline, and show your cowardly face!" shouted the mob.

Cline was hiding in the baggage car. He had been

warned not to appear in Gunn City, but he laughed at the fears of his friends. From the moment the train stopped, he knew he was doomed, and he soon determined to meet his fate boldly. Stepping out upon the platform, he said, —

"Here I am."

A yell went up from the mob, and a volley was fired at him, while he was trying to draw his revolver to defend himself. Pierced by half a dozen bullets, he fell from the platform among his enemies, and expired.

Breaking in the doors and windows of the cars, and threatening to burn the train, the angry mob rushed in among the frightened passengers, yelling, —

"Where are the bond robbers?"

"Turn out the bond thieves!"

Judge Stephenson was discovered in a passenger car. They shot him down and dragged him out upon the grass, where they again fired upon him until he died. Mr. Detro, Cline's bondsman, was the next victim. He was found in the mail car, where he was fired on, and mortally wounded. He was then dragged to the road, and allowed to bleed to death.

Again the mob ran into the train, yelling, —

"Where is General Shelby? Where is Jo Shelby?"

General Shelby, who had not moved from his seat, coolly answered, —

"Here I am; if you want me, come and get me."

His tone and manner were so defiant that they decided to leave him alone. The only excuse the mob could have had for molesting General Shelby was that he had been engaged as counsel for some of the accused officials.

Governor Brown and the State authorities made every effort to bring the murderers to justice, but in vain. They were never identified.

The summary manner in which these bond swindlers were punished put a check upon the reckless issue of bonds by counties. It is certain that the railroad craze in Missouri was carried much too far. Great good has resulted from the numerous railroads built in the State, but many counties heaped up debts that future generations of taxpayers will have to liquidate.

* * * * * * * *

Railroads were not the only improvements following close on the heels of peace. Manufactures of almost every kind started up in the State. Woolen mills, cotton mills, boot and shoe factories, hat factories, small and large, were put in operation all over Missouri.

Mining for iron, lead, zinc, and coal was resumed, among the many other industries, and it seemed as if the metal age had come. The iron industries were pushed to a greater extent than ever before. The Iron Mountain and Pilot Knob iron works were put in operation shortly after the close of the war, and rolling mills and iron mills were started, which have done a prosperous business ever since. Missouri iron has long been in competition with the Pittsburg iron, and for many years large quantities of it were shipped to Indiana, Ohio, and many other States east, south, and west. With her inexhaustible mines, Missouri is capable of competing with the world in the iron industry.

Among the improvements begun soon after the war was the construction of a gigantic bridge across the Mississippi River at St. Louis, to accommodate foot passengers, horses, vehicles, and railway trains. On October 27, 1869, the eastern pier of the bridge was laid with imposing ceremonies.

In order to lay the piers on solid rock in the bottom of the river, great water-tight boxes or caissons were made. These were sunk in the water at the places where the piers were to be, until the lower edges were deep in the muddy bottom.

Steam pumps were then set to work, to pump the water out of the caissons. When this was accomplished, men dug down under them until they came to a rock bed. On the solid rock, they laid the foundation of the great piers, made of massive stones which the current could not carry away.

This work was not only laborious, but also dangerous. Several men lost their lives from poisonous gases which gathered in the caissons, or from the breaking of machinery. But despite all danger and accidents the work was pushed on to completion. Mr. James B. Eads was the architect who planned the wonderful structure, and it is sometimes spoken of as the Eads Bridge. It was completed and formally opened on July 4, 1874; and until 1890, when the Merchants' Bridge was finished, St. Louis had no other bridge across the Mississippi.

* * * * * * * *

With the return of prosperity came a revival of interest in education. The State University at Columbia was the only State educational institution before the war. Soon after peace was restored, Major J. B. Merwin, of the *American Journal of Education*, began advocating a State agricultural college, and a school of mines. He rallied about him able support, and brought such influence to bear on the Legislature, that in 1870 it established the Agricultural College at Columbia, and the School of Mines and Metallurgy at Rolla.

Professor Joseph Baldwin, an able educator just in the prime of life, came from Pennsylvania to Missouri about the year 1867. Aided by Professors J. M. Greenwood, W. P. Nason, S. M. Pickler, Miss Fluhart, Miss Sue Thatcher, and others, he established a private normal school at Kirksville, for the purpose of educating and training teachers. The venture proved such a success that in 1870 the Legislature established three State normal schools, — one at Kirksville, one at Warrensburg, and one at Cape Girardeau, — and also the Lincoln Institute at Jefferson City, for the education of colored teachers. The educational system of Missouri is to-day the equal of that of any State in the Union.

* * * * * * * *

Missouri is a remarkable State. Though not admitted to the Union till 1820, it now ranks fifth in population. The inhabitants to-day number three millions; but this is only a tenth of the population which the State is capable of supporting. If Missouri were cut off from all the remainder of the world, it has natural resources within its own borders sufficient to supply thirty million inhabitants with all the necessaries and comforts essential to a civilized people.

Though there have been panics and failures in all parts of the world, they have merely checked the prosperity of Missouri. That prosperity has never come to a standstill, and to-day no State has a more promising future.

Typography by J. S. Cushing & Co., Norwood, Mass.

www.ingramcontent.com/pod-product-compliance
Lightning Source LLC
Chambersburg PA
CBHW032105220426
43664CB00008B/1137